Oliver Wendell Holmes

Songs in many Keys

Oliver Wendell Holmes

Songs in many Keys

ISBN/EAN: 9783743328655

Manufactured in Europe, USA, Canada, Australia, Japa

Cover: Foto ©ninafisch / pixelio.de

Manufactured and distributed by brebook publishing software (www.brebook.com)

Oliver Wendell Holmes

Songs in many Keys

SONGS IN MANY KEYS.

BY

OLIVER WENDELL HOLMES.

BOSTON:
TICKNOR AND FIELDS.
1862.

Entered according to Act of Congress, in the year 1861, by
OLIVER WENDELL HOLMES,
in the Clerk's Office of the District Court of the District of Massachusetts.

University Press, Cambridge:
Stereotyped and Printed by Welch, Bigelow, & Co.

TO

THE MOST INDULGENT OF READERS,

THE KINDEST OF CRITICS,

MY BELOVED MOTHER,

ALL THAT IS LEAST UNWORTHY OF HER

IN THIS VOLUME

Is Dedicated

BY HER AFFECTIONATE SON.

The piping of our slender, peaceful reeds
Whispers uncared for while the trumpets bray;
Song is thin air; our hearts' exulting play
Beats time but to the tread of marching deeds,
Following the mighty van that Freedom leads,
Her glorious standard flaming to the day!
The crimsoned pavement where a hero bleeds
Breathes nobler lessons than the poet's lay.
Strong arms, broad breasts, brave hearts, are better worth
Than strains that sing the ravished echoes dumb.
Hark! 't is the loud reverberating drum
Rolls o'er the prairied West, the rock-bound North:
The myriad-handed Future stretches forth
Its shadowy palms. Behold, we come, — we come!

Turn o'er these idle leaves. Such toys as these
Were not unsought for, as, in languid dreams,
We lay beside our lotus-feeding streams,
And nursed our fancies in forgetful ease.
It matters little if they pall or please,
Dropping untimely, while the sudden gleams
Glare from the mustering clouds whose blackness seems
Too swollen to hold its lightning from the trees.
Yet, in some lull of passion, when at last
These calm revolving moons that come and go —
Turning our months to years, they creep so slow —
Have brought us rest, the not unwelcome past
May flutter to thee through these leaflets, cast
On the wild winds that all around us blow.

MAY 1st, 1861.

CONTENTS.

	PAGE
AGNES.	
PART I. THE KNIGHT	1
PART II. THE MAIDEN	5
PART III. THE CONQUEST.	13
PART IV. THE RESCUE.	17
PART V. THE REWARD	22
PART VI. CONCLUSION	26
THE PLOUGHMAN	32
A POEM FOR THE DEDICATION OF THE PITTSFIELD CEMETERY	35
PICTURES FROM OCCASIONAL POEMS.	
SPRING	41
THE STUDY.	44
THE BELLS	48
NON-RESISTANCE.	50
THE MORAL BULLY	51
THE MIND'S DIET	53
OUR LIMITATIONS	55
THE OLD PLAYER	56
THE ISLAND RUIN	61
THE BANKER'S DINNER	67
THE MYSTERIOUS ILLNESS	75

A Mother's Secret	79
The Disappointed Statesman	84
The Secret of the Stars	87
To Governor Swain	91
To an English Friend	94
Vignettes.	
After a Lecture on Wordsworth	96
After a Lecture on Moore	101
After a Lecture on Keats	104
After a Lecture on Shelley	106
At the Close of a Course of Lectures	108
The Hudson	110
A Poem for the Meeting of the American Medical Association	112
The New Eden	117
A Sentiment	124
Semicentennial Celebration of the New England Society	125
Ode for Washington's Birthday	128
Class of '29	131
For the Meeting of the Burns Club	133
For the Burns Centennial Celebration	136
Birthday of Daniel Webster	140
Meeting of the Alumni of Harvard College	144
The Parting Song	151
Boston Common. — Three Pictures	153
Latter-Day Warnings	156
Prologue	159
The Old Man of the Sea	163
Ode for a Social Meeting, with Slight Alterations by a Teetotaler	166

CONTENTS.

The Deacon's Masterpiece: or the Wonderful "One-Hoss Shay"	167
Æstivation	173
Contentment	174
Parson Turell's Legacy	178
De Sauty	186
The Old Man dreams	189
Mare Rubrum	192
What we all think	195
Spring has come	198
A Good Time going!	202
The Last Blossom	205
"The Boys"	208
The Opening of the Piano	211
Midsummer	214
A Parting Health. To J. L. Motley	216
A Good-by. To J. R. Lowell	218
At a Birthday Festival. To J. R. Lowell	220
A Birthday Tribute. To J. F. Clarke	222
The Gray Chief	224
The Last Look	226
In Memory of Charles Wentworth Upham, Junior	229
Martha	232
Sun and Shadow	234
The Chambered Nautilus	236
The Two Armies	238
For the Meeting of the National Sanitary Association	241
Musa	244
The Voiceless	248
The Crooked Footpath	250

THE TWO STREAMS	253
ROBINSON OF LEYDEN	255
SAINT ANTHONY THE REFORMER	258
AVIS	260
IRIS, HER BOOK	264
UNDER THE VIOLETS	267
THE PROMISE	270
THE LIVING TEMPLE	272
HYMN OF TRUST	275
A SUN-DAY HYMN	277
A VOICE OF THE LOYAL NORTH	279
BROTHER JONATHAN'S LAMENT FOR SISTER CAROLINE	282
UNDER THE WASHINGTON ELM, CAMBRIDGE	285
INTERNATIONAL ODE	287
FREEDOM, OUR QUEEN	289
ARMY HYMN	291
PARTING HYMN	293
THE FLOWER OF LIBERTY	295
THE SWEET LITTLE MAN	297
VIVE LA FRANCE!	301
UNION AND LIBERTY	304
NOTE TO AGNES	307

AGNES.

PART FIRST.

THE KNIGHT.

The tale I tell is gospel true,
    As all the bookmen know,
And pilgrims who have strayed to view
    The wrecks still left to show.

The old, old story, — fair, and young,
    And fond, — and not too wise, —
That matrons tell, with sharpened tongue,
    To maids with downcast eyes.

Ah! maidens err and matrons warn
    Beneath the coldest sky;
Love lurks amid the tasselled corn
    As in the bearded rye!

But who would dream our sober sires
    Had learned the old world's ways,
And warmed their hearths with lawless fires
    In Shirley's homespun days?

'T is like some poet's pictured trance
    His idle rhymes recite, —
This old New-England-born romance
    Of Agnes and the Knight;

Yet, known to all the country round,
    Their home is standing still,
Between Wachusett's lonely mound
    And Shawmut's threefold hill.

— One hour we rumble on the rail,
    One half-hour guide the rein,
We reach at last, o'er hill and dale,
    The village on the plain.

With blackening wall and mossy roof,
    With stained and warping floor,
A stately mansion stands aloof
    And bars its haughty door.

This lowlier portal may be tried,
    That breaks the gable wall;
And lo! with arches opening wide,
    Sir Harry Frankland's hall!

'T was in the second George's day
    They sought the forest shade,
The knotted trunks they cleared away,
    The massive beams they laid,

They piled the rock-hewn chimney tall,
    They smoothed the terraced ground,
They reared the marble-pillared wall
    That fenced the mansion round.

Far stretched beyond the village bound
    The Master's broad domain;
With page and valet, horse and hound,
    He kept a goodly train.

And, all the midland county through,
    The ploughman stopped to gaze
Whenc'er his chariot swept in view
    Behind the shining bays,

With mute obeisance, grave and slow,
    Repaid by nod polite, —
For such the way with high and low
    Till after Concord fight.

Nor less to courtly circles known
    That graced the three-hilled town
With far-off splendors of the Throne,
    And glimmerings from the Crown;

Wise Phipps, who held the seals of state
    For Shirley over sea;
Brave Knowles, whose press-gang moved of late
    The King Street mob's decree;

And judges grave, and colonels grand,
    Fair dames and stately men,
The mighty people of the land,
    The "World" of there and then.

'T was strange no Chloe's "beauteous Form,"
    And "Eyes' cœlestial Blew,"
This Strephon of the West could warm,
    No Nymph his Heart subdue!

Perchance he wooed as gallants use,
    Whom fleeting loves enchain,
But still unfettered, free to choose,
    Would brook no bridle-rein.

He saw the fairest of the fair,
    But smiled alike on all;
No band his roving foot might snare,
    No ring his hand enthrall.

PART SECOND.

THE MAIDEN.

Why seeks the knight that rocky cape
    Beyond the Bay of Lynn?
What chance his wayward course may shape
    To reach its village inn?

No story tells; whate'er we guess,
    The past lies deaf and still,
But Fate, who rules to blight or bless,
    Can lead us where she will.

Make way! Sir Harry's coach and four,
    And liveried grooms that ride!
They cross the ferry, touch the shore
    On Winnisimmet's side.

They hear the wash on Chelsea Beach, —
    The level marsh they pass,
Where miles on miles the desert reach
    Is rough with bitter grass.

The shining horses foam and pant,
    And now the smells begin
Of fishy Swampscot, salt Nahant,
    And leather-scented Lynn.

Next, on their left, the slender spires,
    And glittering vanes, that crown
The home of Salem's frugal sires,
    The old, witch-haunted town.

So onward, o'er the rugged way
    That runs through rocks and sand,
Showered by the tempest-driven spray,
    From bays on either hand,

That shut between their outstretched arms
    The crews of Marblehead,
The lords of ocean's watery farms,
    Who plough the waves for bread.

At last the ancient inn appears,
    The spreading elm below,
Whose flapping sign these fifty years
    Has seesawed to and fro.

How fair the azure fields in sight
    Before the low-browed inn !
The tumbling billows fringe with light
    The crescent shore of Lynn ;

Nahant thrusts outward through the waves
    Her arm of yellow sand,
And breaks the roaring surge that braves
    The gauntlet on her hand ;

With eddying whirl the waters lock
    Yon treeless mound forlorn,
The sharp-winged sea-fowl's breeding-rock,
    That fronts the Spouting Horn ;

Then free the white-sailed shallops glide,
    And wide the ocean smiles,
Till, shoreward bent, his streams divide
    The two bare Misery Isles.

The master's silent signal stays
    The wearied cavalcade;
The coachman reins his smoking bays
    Beneath the elm-tree's shade.

A gathering on the village green!
    The cocked-hats crowd to see,
On legs in ancient velveteen,
    With buckles at the knee!

A clustering round the tavern-door
    Of square-toed village boys,
Still wearing, as their grandsires wore,
    The old-world corduroys!

A scampering at the "Fountain" inn, —
    A rush of great and small, —
With hurrying servants' mingled din
    And screaming matron's call!

AGNES.

Poor Agnes! with her work half done
    They caught her unaware;
As, humbly, like a praying nun,
    She knelt upon the stair;

Bent o'er the steps, with lowliest mien
    She knelt, but not to pray, —
Her little hands must keep them clean,
    And wash their stains away.

A foot, an ankle, bare and white
    Her girlish shapes betrayed, —
"Ha! Nymphs and Graces!" spoke the Knight;
    "Look up, my beauteous Maid!"

She turned, — a reddening rose in bud,
    Its calyx half withdrawn, —
Her cheek on fire with damasked blood
    Of girlhood's glowing dawn!

He searched her features through and through,
    As royal lovers look
On lowly maidens, when they woo
    Without the ring and book.

"Come hither, Fair one! Here, my Sweet!
 Nay, prithee, look not down!
Take this to shoe those little feet," —
 He tossed a silver crown.

A sudden paleness struck her brow, —
 A swifter flush succeeds;
It burns her cheek; it kindles now
 Beneath her golden beads.

She flitted, but the glittering eye
 Still sought the lovely face.
Who was she? What, and whence? and why
 Doomed to such menial place?

A skipper's daughter, — so they said, —
 Left orphan by the gale
That cost the fleet of Marblehead
 And Gloucester thirty sail.

Ah! many a lonely home is found
 Along the Essex shore,
That cheered its goodman outward bound,
 And sees his face no more!

"Not so," the matron whispered, — " sure
    No orphan girl is she, —
The Surraige folk are deadly poor
    Since Edward left the sea,

"And Mary, with her growing brood,
    Has work enough to do
To find the children clothes and food
    With Thomas, John, and Hugh.

"This girl of Mary's, growing tall, —
    (Just turned her sixteenth year,) —
To earn her bread and help them all,
    Would work as housemaid here."

So Agnes, with her golden beads,
    And naught beside as dower,
Grew at the wayside with the weeds,
    Herself a garden-flower.

'T was strange, 't was sad, — so fresh, so fair !
    Thus Pity's voice began.
Such grace! an angel's shape and air!
    The half-heard whisper ran.

For eyes could see in George's time,
    As now in later days,
And lips could shape, in prose and rhyme,
    The honeyed breath of praise.

No time to woo! The train must go
    Long ere the sun is down,
To reach, before the night-winds blow,
    The many-steepled town.

'T is midnight, — street and square are still;
    Dark roll the whispering waves
That lap the piers beneath the hill
    Ridged thick with ancient graves.

Ah, gentle sleep! thy hand will smooth
    The weary couch of pain,
When all thy poppies fail to soothe
    The lover's throbbing brain!

'T is morn, — the orange-mantled sun
    Breaks through the fading gray,
And long and loud the Castle gun
    Peals o'er the glistening bay.

"Thank God 't is day!" With eager eye
   He hails the morning's shine: —
"If art can win, or gold can buy,
   The maiden shall be mine!"

PART THIRD.

THE CONQUEST.

"Who saw this hussy when she came?
   What is the wench, and who?"
They whisper. "*Agnes*, — is her name?
   Pray what has she to do?"

The housemaids parley at the gate,
   The scullions on the stair,
And in the footmen's grave debate
   The butler deigns to share.

Black Dinah, stolen when a child,
   And sold on Boston pier,
Grown up in service, petted, spoiled,
   Speaks in the coachman's ear:

"What, all this household at his will?
  And all are yet too few?
More servants, and more servants still, —
  This pert young madam too!"

"*Servant!* fine servant!" laughed aloud
  The man of coach and steeds;
"She looks too fair, she steps too proud,
  This girl with golden beads!

"I tell you, you may fret and frown,
  And call her what you choose,
You 'll find my Lady in her gown,
  Your Mistress in her shoes!"

Ah, gentle maidens, free from blame,
  God grant you never know
The little whisper, loud with shame,
  That makes the world your foe!

Why tell the lordly flatterer's art,
  That won the maiden's ear, —
The fluttering of the frightened heart,
  The blush, the smile, the tear?

Alas! it were the saddening tale
    That every language knows, —
The wooing wind, the yielding sail,
    The sunbeam and the rose.

And now the gown of sober stuff
    Has changed to fair brocade,
With broidered hem, and hanging cuff,
    And flower of silken braid;

And clasped around her blanching wrist
    A jewelled bracelet shines,
Her flowing tresses' massive twist
    A glittering net confines;

And mingling with their truant wave
    A fretted chain is hung;
But ah! the gift her mother gave, —
    Its beads are all unstrung!

Her place is at the master's board,
    Where none disputes her claim;
She walks beside the mansion's lord,
    His bride in all but name.

The busy tongues have ceased to talk,
   Or speak in softened tone,
So gracious in her daily walk
   The angel light has shown.

No want that kindness may relieve
   Assails her heart in vain,
The lifting of a ragged sleeve
   Will check her palfrey's rein.

A thoughtful calm, a quiet grace
   In every movement shown,
Reveal her moulded for the place
   She may not call her own.

And, save that on her youthful brow
   There broods a shadowy care,
No matron sealed with holy vow
   In all the land so fair!

PART FOURTH.

THE RESCUE.

A SHIP comes foaming up the bay,
    Along the pier she glides ;
Before her furrow melts away,
    A courier mounts and rides.

"Haste, Haste, post Haste!" the letters bear;
    "Sir Harry Frankland, These."
Sad news to tell the loving pair!
    The knight must cross the seas.

"Alas! we part!" — the lips that spoke
    Lost all their rosy red,
As when a crystal cup is broke,
    And all its wine is shed.

"Nay, droop not thus, — where'er," he cried,
    "I go by land or sea,
My love, my life, my joy, my pride,
    Thy place is still by me!"

Through town and city, far and wide,
    Their wandering feet have strayed,
From Alpine lake to ocean tide,
    And cold Sierra's shade.

At length they see the waters gleam
    Amid the fragrant bowers
Where Lisbon mirrors in the stream
    Her belt of ancient towers.

Red is the orange on its bough,
    To-morrow's sun shall fling
O'er Cintra's hazel-shaded brow
    The flush of April's wing.

The streets are loud with noisy mirth,
    They dance on every green;
The morning's dial marks the birth
    Of proud Braganza's queen.

At eve beneath their pictured dome
    The gilded courtiers throng;
The broad moidores have cheated Rome
    Of all her lords of song.

Ah! Lisbon dreams not of the day —
    Pleased with her painted scenes —
When all her towers shall slide away
    As now these canvas screens!

The spring has passed, the summer fled,
    And yet they linger still,
Though autumn's rustling leaves have spread
    The flank of Cintra's hill.

The town has learned their Saxon name,
    And touched their English gold,
Nor tale of doubt nor hint of blame
    From over sea is told.

Three hours the first November dawn
    Has climbed with feeble ray
Through mists like heavy curtains drawn
    Before the darkened day.

How still the muffled echoes sleep!
    Hark! hark! a hollow sound, —
A noise like chariots rumbling deep

The channel lifts, the water slides
    And bares its bar of sand,
Anon a mountain billow strides
    And crashes o'er the land.

The turrets lean, the steeples reel
    Like masts on ocean's swell,
And clash a long discordant peal,
    The death-doomed city's knell.

The pavement bursts, the earth upheaves
    Beneath the staggering town!
The turrets crack — the castle cleaves —
    The spires come rushing down.

Around, the lurid mountains glow
    With strange unearthly gleams;
While black abysses gape below,
    Then close in jagged seams.

The earth has folded like a wave,
    And thrice a thousand score,
Clasped, shroudless, in their closing grave,
    The sun shall see no more!

And all is over. Street and square
  In ruined heaps are piled;
Ah! where is she, so frail, so fair,
  Amid the tumult wild?

Unscathed, she treads the wreck-piled street,
  Whose narrow gaps afford
A pathway for her bleeding feet,
  To seek her absent lord.

A temple's broken walls arrest
  Her wild and wandering eyes;
Beneath its shattered portal pressed,
  Her lord unconscious lies.

The power that living hearts obey
  Shall lifeless blocks withstand?
Love led her footsteps where he lay, —
  Love nerves her woman's hand:

One cry, — the marble shaft she grasps, —
  Up heaves the ponderous stone: —
He breathes, — her fainting form he clasps, —
  Her life has bought his own!

PART FIFTH.

THE REWARD.

How like the starless night of death
    Our being's brief eclipse,
When faltering heart and failing breath
    Have bleached the fading lips!

She lives! What guerdon shall repay
    His debt of ransomed life?
One word can charm all wrongs away, —
    The sacred name of WIFE!

The love that won her girlish charms
    Must shield her matron fame,
And write beneath the Frankland arms
    The village beauty's name.

Go, call the priest! no vain delay
    Shall dim the sacred ring!
Who knows what change the passing day,
    The fleeting hour, may bring?

Before the holy altar bent,
  There kneels a goodly pair;
A stately man, of high descent,
  A woman, passing fair.

No jewels lend the blinding sheen
  That meaner beauty needs,
But on her bosom heaves unseen
  A string of golden beads.

The vow is spoke, — the prayer is said, —
  And with a gentle pride
The Lady Agnes lifts her head,
  Sir Harry Frankland's bride.

No more her faithful heart shall bear
  Those griefs so meekly borne, —
The passing sneer, the freezing stare,
  The icy look of scorn;

No more the blue-eyed English dames
  Their haughty lips shall curl,
Whene'er a hissing whisper names
  The poor New-England girl.

But stay! — his mother's haughty brow, —
    The pride of ancient race, —
Will plighted faith, and holy vow,
    Win back her fond embrace?

Too well she knew the saddening tale
    Of love no vow had blest,
That turned his blushing honors pale
    And stained his knightly crest.

They seek his Northern home, — alas!
    He goes alone before; —
His own dear Agnes may not pass
    The proud, ancestral door.

He stood before the stately dame;
    He spoke; she calmly heard,
But not to pity, nor to blame;
    She breathed no single word.

He told his love, — her faith betrayed;
    She heard with tearless eyes;
Could she forgive the erring maid?
    She stared in cold surprise.

How fond her heart, he told, — how true ;
  The haughty eyelids fell ; —
The kindly deeds she loved to do ;
  She murmured, " It is well."

But when he told that fearful day,
  And how her feet were led
To where entombed in life he lay,
  The breathing with the dead,

And how she bruised her tender breasts
  Against the crushing stone,
That still the strong-armed clown protests
  No man can lift alone, —

O then the frozen spring was broke ;
  By turns she wept and smiled ; —
" Sweet Agnes ! " so the mother spoke,
  " God bless my angel child !

" She saved thee from the jaws of death, —
  'T is thine to right her wrongs ;
I tell thee, — I, who gave thee breath, —
  To her thy life belongs ! "

Thus Agnes won her noble name,
    Her lawless lover's hand;
The lowly maiden so became
    A lady in the land!

PART SIXTH.

CONCLUSION.

The tale is done; it little needs
    To track their after ways,
And string again the golden beads
    Of love's uncounted days.

They leave the fair ancestral isle
    For bleak New England's shore;
How gracious is the courtly smile
    Of all who frowned before!

Again through Lisbon's orange bowers
    They watch the river's gleam,
And shudder as her shadowy towers
    Shake in the trembling stream.

Fate parts at length the fondest pair;
    His cheek, alas! grows pale;
The breast that trampling death could spare
    His noiseless shafts assail.

He longs to change the heaven of blue
    For England's clouded sky, —
To breathe the air his boyhood knew;
    He seeks them but to die.

— Hard by the terraced hill-side town,
    Where healing streamlets run,
Still sparkling with their old renown, —
    The "Waters of the Sun," —

The Lady Agnes raised the stone
    That marks his honored grave,
And there Sir Harry sleeps alone
    By Wiltshire Avon's wave.

The home of early love was dear;
    She sought its peaceful shade,
And kept her state for many a year,
    With none to make afraid.

At last the evil days were come
    That saw the red cross fall;
She hears the rebels' rattling drum, —
    Farewell to Frankland Hall!

— I tell you, as my tale began,
    The Hall is standing still;
And you, kind listener, maid or man,
    May see it if you will.

The box is glistening huge and green,
    Like trees the lilacs grow,
Three elms high-arching still are seen,
    And one lies stretched below.

The hangings, rough with velvet flowers,
    Flap on the latticed wall;
And o'er the mossy ridge-pole towers
    The rock-hewn chimney tall.

The doors on mighty hinges clash
    With massive bolt and bar,
The heavy English-moulded sash
    Scarce can the night-winds jar.

Behold the chosen room he sought
    Alone, to fast and pray,
Each year, as chill November brought
    The dismal earthquake day.

There hung the rapier blade he wore,
    Bent in its flattened sheath;
The coat the shrieking woman tore
    Caught in her clenching teeth; —

The coat with tarnished silver lace
    She snapped at as she slid,
And down upon her death-white face
    Crashed the huge coffin's lid.

A graded terrace yet remains;
    If on its turf you stand
And look along the wooded plains
    That stretch on either hand,

The broken forest walls define
    A dim, receding view,
Where, on the far horizon's line
    He cut his vista through.

If further story you shall crave,
    Or ask for living proof,
Go see old Julia, born a slave
    Beneath Sir Harry's roof.

She told me half that I have told,
    And she remembers well
The mansion as it looked of old
    Before its glories fell; —

The box, when round the terraced square
    Its glossy wall was drawn;
The climbing vines, the snow-balls fair,
    The roses on the lawn.

And Julia says, with truthful look
    Stamped on her wrinkled face,
That in her own black hands she took
    The coat with silver lace.

And you may hold the story light,
    Or, if you like, believe;
But there it was, the woman's bite, —
    A mouthful from the sleeve.

Now go your ways: — I need not tell
    The moral of my rhyme;
But, youths and maidens, ponder well,
    This tale of olden time!

THE PLOUGHMAN.

(ANNIVERSARY OF THE BERKSHIRE AGRICULTURAL SOCIETY
OCT. 4, 1849.)

CLEAR the brown path, to meet his coulter's gleam!
Lo! on he comes, behind his smoking team,
With toil's bright dew-drops on his sunburnt brow,
The lord of earth, the hero of the plough!

First in the field before the reddening sun,
Last in the shadows when the day is done,
Line after line, along the bursting sod,
Marks the broad acres where his feet have trod;
Still, where he treads, the stubborn clods divide,
The smooth, fresh furrow opens deep and wide;
Matted and dense the tangled turf upheaves,
Mellow and dark the ridgy cornfield cleaves;
Up the steep hill-side, where the laboring train
Slants the long track that scores the level plain;

Through the moist valley, clogged with oozing clay,
The patient convoy breaks its destined way;
At every turn the loosening chains resound,
The swinging ploughshare circles glistening round,
Till the wide field one billowy waste appears,
And wearied hands unbind the panting steers.

These are the hands whose sturdy labor brings
The peasant's food, the golden pomp of kings:
This is the page, whose letters shall be seen
Changed by the sun to words of living green;
This is the scholar, whose immortal pen
Spells the first lesson hunger taught to men;
These are the lines that heaven-commanded Toil
Shows on his deed, — the charter of the soil!

O gracious Mother, whose benignant breast
Wakes us to life, and lulls us all to rest,
How thy sweet features, kind to every clime,
Mock with their smile the wrinkled front of time!
We stain thy flowers, — they blossom o'er the dead;
We rend thy bosom, and it gives us bread;
O'er the red field that trampling strife has torn,
Waves the green plumage of thy tasselled corn;

Our maddening conflicts scar thy fairest plain,
Still thy soft answer is the growing grain.
Yet, O our Mother, while uncounted charms
Steal round our hearts in thine embracing arms,
Let not our virtues in thy love decay,
And thy fond sweetness waste our strength away.

No! by these hills, whose banners now displayed
In blazing cohorts Autumn has arrayed:
By yon twin summits, on whose splintery crests
The tossing hemlocks hold the eagle's nests;
By these fair plains the mountain circle screens,
And feeds with streamlets from its dark ravines; —
True to their home, these faithful arms shall toil
To crown with peace their own untainted soil;
And, true to God, to freedom, to mankind,
If her chained bandogs Faction shall unbind,
These stately forms, that bending even now
Bowed their strong manhood to the humble plough,
Shall rise erect, the guardians of the land,
The same stern iron in the same right hand,
'Till o'er their hills the shouts of triumph run;
The sword has rescued what the ploughshare won!

A POEM.

(DEDICATION OF THE PITTSFIELD CEMETERY, SEPTEMBER 9, 1850.)

ANGEL of Death! extend thy silent reign!
Stretch thy dark sceptre o'er this new domain!
No sable car along the winding road
Has borne to earth its unresisting load;
No sudden mound has risen yet to show
Where the pale slumberer folds his arms below;
No marble gleams to bid his memory live
In the brief lines that hurrying Time can give;
Yet, O Destroyer! from thy shrouded throne
Look on our gift; this realm is all thine own!

Fair is the scene; its sweetness oft beguiled
From their dim paths the children of the wild;
The dark-haired maiden loved its grassy dells,
The feathered warrior claimed its wooded swells,

Still on its slopes the ploughman's ridges show
The pointed flints that left his fatal bow,
Chipped with rough art and slow barbarian toil, —
Last of his wrecks that strews the alien soil!

  Here spread the fields that heaped their ripened store
Till the brown arms of Labor held no more;
The scythe's broad meadow with its dusky blush;
The sickle's harvest with its velvet flush;
The green-haired maize, her silken tresses laid,
In soft luxuriance, on her harsh brocade;
The gourd that swells beneath her tossing plume;
The coarser wheat that rolls in lakes of bloom, —
Its coral stems and milk-white flowers alive
With the wide murmurs of the scattered hive;
Here glowed the apple with the pencilled streak
Of morning painted on its southern cheek;
The pear's long necklace strung with golden drops,
Arched, like the banian, o'er its pillared props;
Here crept the growths that paid the laborer's care
With the cheap luxuries wealth consents to spare;
Here sprang the healing herbs which could not save
The hand that reared them from the neighboring grave.

  Yet all its varied charms, forever free
From task and tribute, Labor yields to thee;

No more, when April sheds her fitful rain,
The sower's hand shall cast its flying grain;
No more, when Autumn strews the flaming leaves,
The reaper's band shall gird its yellow sheaves;
For thee alike the circling seasons flow
Till the first blossoms heave the latest snow.
In the stiff clod below the whirling drifts,
In the loose soil the springing herbage lifts,
In the hot dust beneath the parching weeds,
Life's withering flower shall drop its shrivelled seeds;
Its germ entranced in thy unbreathing sleep
Till what thou sowest mightier angels reap!

Spirit of Beauty! let thy graces blend
With loveliest Nature all that Art can lend.
Come from the bowers where Summer's life-blood flows
Through the red lips of June's half-open rose,
Dressed in bright hues, the loving sunshine's dower;
For tranquil Nature owns no mourning flower.
  Come from the forest where the beech's screen
Bars the fierce noonbeam with its flakes of green;
Stay the rude axe that bares the shadowy plains,
Stanch the deep wound that dries the maple's veins.
  Come with the stream whose silver-braided rills
Fling their unclasping bracelets from the hills,

Till in one gleam, beneath the forest's wings,
Melts the white glitter of a hundred springs.

   Come from the steeps where look majestic forth
From their twin thrones the Giants of the North
On the huge shapes, that, crouching at their knees,
Stretch their broad shoulders, rough with shaggy trees.
Through the wide waste of ether, not in vain,
Their softened gaze shall reach our distant plain;
There, while the mourner turns his aching eyes
On the blue mounds that print the bluer skies,
Nature shall whisper that the fading view
Of mightiest grief may wear a heavenly hue.

Cherub of Wisdom! let thy marble page
Leave its sad lesson, new to every age;
Teach us to live, not grudging every breath
To the chill winds that waft us on to death,
But ruling calmly every pulse it warms,
And tempering gently every word it forms.

Seraph of Love! in heaven's adoring zone,
Nearest of all around the central throne,
While with soft hands the pillowed turf we spread
That soon shall hold us in its dreamless bed,
With the low whisper, — Who shall first be laid

In the dark chamber's yet unbroken shade? —
Let thy sweet radiance shine rekindled here,
And all we cherish grow more truly dear.
Here in the gates of Death's o'erhanging vault,
O, teach us kindness for our brother's fault;
Lay all our wrongs beneath this peaceful sod,
And lead our hearts to Mercy and its God.

FATHER of all! in Death's relentless claim
We read thy mercy by its sterner name;
In the bright flower that decks the solemn bier,
We see thy glory in its narrowed sphere;
In the deep lessons that affliction draws,
We trace the curves of thy encircling laws;
In the long sigh that sets our spirits free,
We own the love that calls us back to Thee!

Through the hushed street, along the silent plain,
The spectral future leads its mourning train,
Dark with the shadows of uncounted bands,
Where man's white lips and woman's wringing hands
Track the still burden, rolling slow before,
That love and kindness can protect no more;
The smiling babe that, called to mortal strife,
Shuts its meek eyes and drops its little life;

The drooping child who prays in vain to live,
And pleads for help its parent cannot give;
The pride of beauty stricken in its flower;
The strength of manhood broken in an hour;
Age in its weakness, bowed by toil and care,
Traced in sad lines beneath its silvered hair.

  The sun shall set, and heaven's resplendent spheres
Gild the smooth turf unhallowed yet by tears,
But ah! how soon the evening stars will shed
Their sleepless light around the slumbering dead!

  Take them, O Father, in immortal trust!
Ashes to ashes, dust to kindred dust,
Till the last angel rolls the stone away,
And a new morning brings eternal day!

PICTURES FROM OCCASIONAL POEMS.

1850 – 56.

SPRING.

WINTER is past; the heart of Nature warms
Beneath the wrecks of unresisted storms;
Doubtful at first, suspected more than seen,
The southern slopes are fringed with tender green;
On sheltered banks, beneath the dripping eaves,
Spring's earliest nurslings spread their glowing leaves,
Bright with the hues from wider pictures won,
White, azure, golden, — drift, or sky, or sun; —
The snowdrop, bearing on her patient breast
The frozen trophy torn from Winter's crest;
The violet, gazing on the arch of blue
Till her own iris wears its deepened hue;
The spendthrift crocus, bursting through the mould
Naked and shivering with his cup of gold.
Swelled with new life, the darkening elm on high
Prints her thick buds against the spotted sky;

On all her boughs the stately chestnut cleaves
The gummy shroud that wraps her embryo leaves;
The house-fly, stealing from his narrow grave,
Drugged with the opiate that November gave,
Beats with faint wing against the sunny pane,
Or crawls, tenacious, o'er its lucid plain;
From shaded chinks of lichen-crusted walls,
In languid curves, the gliding serpent crawls;
The bog's green harper, thawing from his sleep,
Twangs a hoarse note and tries a shortened leap;
On floating rails that face the softening noons
The still shy turtles range their dark platoons,
Or, toiling aimless o'er the mellowing fields,
Trail through the grass their tessellated shields.

At last young April, ever frail and fair,
Wooed by her playmate with the golden hair,
Chased to the margin of receding floods
O'er the soft meadows starred with opening buds,
In tears and blushes sighs herself away,
And hides her cheek beneath the flowers of May.

Then the proud tulip lights her beacon blaze,
Her clustering curls the hyacinth displays,

O'er her tall blades the crested fleur-de-lis,
Like blue-eyed Pallas, towers erect and free;
With yellower flames the lengthened sunshine glows,
And love lays bare the passion-breathing rose;
Queen of the lake, along its reedy verge
The rival lily hastens to emerge,
Her snowy shoulders glistening as she strips,
Till morn is sultan of her parted lips.

Then bursts the song from every leafy glade,
The yielding season's bridal serenade;
Then flash the wings returning Summer calls
Through the deep arches of her forest halls;—
The bluebird, breathing from his azure plumes
The fragrance borrowed where the myrtle blooms;
The thrush, poor wanderer, dropping meekly down,
Clad in his remnant of autumnal brown;
The oriole, drifting like a flake of fire
Rent by the whirlwind from a blazing spire.
The robin, jerking his spasmodic throat,
Repeats, imperious, his *staccáto* note;
The crack-brained bobolink courts his crazy mate,
Poised on a bulrush tipsy with his weight;
Nay, in his cage the lone canary sings,
Feels the soft air, and spreads his idle wings.

Why dream I here within these caging walls,
Deaf to her voice, while blooming Nature calls;
Peering and gazing with insatiate looks
Through blinding lenses, or in wearying books?
Off, gloomy spectres of the shrivelled past!
Fly with the leaves that filled the autumn blast!
Ye imps of Science, whose relentless chains
Lock the warm tides within these living veins,
Close your dim cavern, while its captive strays
Dazzled and giddy in the morning's blaze!

THE STUDY.

YET in the darksome crypt I left so late,
Whose only altar is its rusted grate, —
Sepulchral, rayless, joyless as it seems,
Shamed by the glare of May's refulgent beams, —
While the dim seasons dragged their shrouded train,
Its paler splendors were not quite in vain.
From these dull bars the cheerful firelight's glow
Streamed through the casement o'er the spectral snow;
Here, while the night-wind wreaked its frantic will
On the loose ocean and the rock-bound hill,
Rent the cracked topsail from its quivering yard,
And rived the oak a thousand storms had scarred,

Fenced by these walls the peaceful taper shone,
Nor felt a breath to slant its trembling cone.

Not all unblest the mild interior scene
When the red curtain spread its falling screen;
O'er some light task the lonely hours were past,
And the long evening only flew too fast;
Or the wide chair its leathern arms would lend
In genial welcome to some easy friend,
Stretched on its bosom with relaxing nerves,
Slow moulding, plastic, to its hollow curves;
Perchance indulging, if of generous creed,
In brave Sir Walter's dream-compelling weed.
Or, happier still, the evening hour would bring
To the round table its expected ring,
And while the punch-bowl's sounding depths were
    stirred, —
Its silver cherubs smiling as they heard, —
Our hearts would open, as at evening's hour
The close-sealed primrose frees its hidden flower.

Such the warm life this dim retreat has known,
Not quite deserted when its guests were flown;
Nay, filled with friends, an unobtrusive set,
Guiltless of calls and cards and etiquette,

Ready to answer, never known to ask,
Claiming no service, prompt for every task.

On those dark shelves no housewife hand profanes,
O'er his mute files the monarch folio reigns;
A mingled race, the wreck of chance and time,
That talk all tongues and breathe of every clime;
Each knows his place, and each may claim his part
In some quaint corner of his master's heart.
This old Decretal, won from Kloss's hoards,
Thick-leaved, brass-cornered, ribbed with oaken boards,
Stands the gray patriarch of the graver rows,
Its fourth ripe century narrowing to its close;
Not daily conned, but glorious still to view,
With glistening letters wrought in red and blue.
There towers Stagira's all-embracing sage,
The Aldine anchor on his opening page;
There sleep the births of Plato's heavenly mind,
In yon dark tomb by jealous clasps confined,
" Olim e libris " — (dare I call it mine?)
Of Yale's grave Head and Killingworth's divine!
In those square sheets the songs of Maro fill
The silvery types of smooth-leaved Baskerville;
High over all, in close, compact array,
Their classic wealth the Elzevirs display.

In lower regions of the sacred space
Range the dense volumes of a humbler race;
There grim chirurgeons all their mysteries teach
In spectral pictures, or in crabbed speech;
Harvey and Haller, fresh from Nature's page,
Shoulder the dreamers of an earlier age,
Lully and Geber, and the learned crew
That loved to talk of all they could not do.
Why count the rest, — those names of later days
That many love, and all agree to praise, —
Or point the titles, where a glance may read
The dangerous lines of party or of creed?
Too well, perchance, the chosen list would show
What few may care and none can claim to know.
Each has his features, whose exterior seal
A brush may copy, or a sunbeam steal;
Go to his study, — on the nearest shelf
Stands the mosaic portrait of himself.

What though for months the tranquil dust descends,
Whitening the heads of these mine ancient friends,
While the damp offspring of the modern press
Flaunts on my table with its pictured dress;
Not less I love each dull familiar face,
Nor less should miss it from the appointed place;

I snatch the book, along whose burning leaves
His scarlet web our wild romancer weaves,
Yet, while proud Hester's fiery pangs I share,
My old MAGNALIA must be standing *there!*

THE BELLS.

WHEN o'er the street the morning peal is flung
From yon tall belfry with the brazen tongue,
Its wide vibrations, wafted by the gale,
To each far listener tell a different tale.

 The sexton, stooping to the quivering floor
Till the great caldron spills its brassy roar,
Whirls the hot axle, counting, one by one,
Each dull concussion, till his task is done.

 Toil's patient daughter, when the welcome note
Clangs through the silence from the steeple's throat,
Streams, a white unit, to the checkered street,
Demure, but guessing whom she soon shall meet;
The bell, responsive to her secret flame,
With every note repeats her lover's name.

 The lover, tenant of the neighboring lane,
Sighing, and fearing lest he sigh in vain,
Hears the stern accents, as they come and go,
Their only burden one despairing No!

Ocean's rough child, whom many a shore has known
Ere homeward breezes swept him to his own,
Starts at the echo as it circles round,
A thousand memories kindling with the sound;
The early favorite's unforgotten charms,
Whose blue initials stain his tawny arms;
His first farewell, the flapping canvas spread,
The seaward streamers crackling o'er his head,
His kind, pale mother, not ashamed to weep
Her first-born's bridal with the haggard deep,
While the brave father stood with tearless eye,
Smiling and choking with his last good by.

'T is but a wave, whose spreading circle beats,
With the same impulse, every nerve it meets,
Yet who shall count the varied shapes that ride
On the round surge of that aerial tide !

O child of earth ! If floating sounds like these
Steal from thyself their power to wound or please,
If here or there thy changing will inclines,
As the bright zodiac shifts its rolling signs,
Look at thy heart, and when its depths are known,
Then try thy brother's, judging by thine own,

But keep thy wisdom to the narrower range,
While its own standards are the sport of change,
Nor count us rebels when we disobey
The passing breath that holds thy passion's sway.

NON-RESISTANCE.

Perhaps too far in these considerate days
Has patience carried her submissive ways;
Wisdom has taught us to be calm and meek,
To take one blow, and turn the other cheek;
It is not written what a man shall do,
If the rude caitiff strike the other too!

Land of our fathers, in thine hour of need
God help thee, guarded by the passive creed!
As the lone pilgrim trusts to beads and cowl,
When through the forest rings the gray wolf's howl
As the deep galleon trusts her gilded prow
When the black corsair slants athwart her bow;
As the poor pheasant, with his peaceful mien,
Trusts to his feathers, shining golden-green,
When the dark plumage with the crimson beak
Has rustled shadowy from its splintered peak;

So trust thy friends, whose babbling tongues would charm
The lifted sabre from thy foeman's arm,
Thy torches ready for the answering peal
From bellowing fort and thunder-freighted keel!

THE MORAL BULLY.

Yon whey-faced brother, who delights to wear
A weedy flux of ill-conditioned hair,
Seems of the sort that in a crowded place
One elbows freely into smallest space;
A timid creature, lax of knee and hip,
Whom small disturbance whitens round the lip;
One of those harmless spectacled machines,
The Holy-Week of Protestants convenes;
Whom schoolboys question if their walk transcends
The last advices of maternal friends;
Whom John, obedient to his master's sign,
Conducts, laborious, up to *ninety-nine*,
While Peter, glistening with luxurious scorn,
Husks his white ivories like an ear of corn;
Dark in the brow and bilious in the cheek,
Whose yellowish linen flowers but once a week,
Conspicuous, annual, in their threadbare suits,

And the laced high-lows which they call their boots.
Well mayst thou *shun* that dingy front severe,
But him, O stranger, him thou canst not *fear!*

Be slow to judge, and slower to despise,
Man of broad shoulders and heroic size!
The tiger, writhing from the boa's rings,
Drops at the fountain where the cobra stings.
In that lean phantom, whose extended glove
Points to the text of universal love,
Behold the master that can tame thee down
To crouch, the vassal of his Sunday frown;
His velvet throat against thy corded wrist,
His loosened tongue against thy doubled fist!

The MORAL BULLY, though he never swears,
Nor kicks intruders down his entry stairs,
Though meekness plants his backward-sloping hat,
And non-resistance ties his white cravat,
Though his black broadcloth glories to be seen
In the same plight with Shylock's gaberdine,
Hugs the same passion to his narrow breast
That heaves the cuirass on the trooper's chest,
Hears the same hell-hounds yelling in his rear
That chase from port the maddened buccaneer,

Feels the same comfort while his acrid words
Turn the sweet milk of kindness into curds,
Or with grim logic prove, beyond debate,
That all we love is worthiest of our hate,
As the scarred ruffian of the pirate's deck,
When his long swivel rakes the staggering wreck!

Heaven keep us all! Is every rascal clown
Whose arm is stronger free to knock us down?
Has every scarecrow, whose cachectic soul
Seems fresh from Bedlam, airing on parole,
Who, though he carries but a doubtful trace
Of angel visits on his hungry face,
From lack of marrow or the coins to pay,
Has dodged some vices in a shabby way,
The right to stick us with his cut-throat terms,
And bait his homilies with his brother worms?

THE MIND'S DIET.

No life worth naming ever comes to good
If always nourished on the self-same food;
The creeping mite may live so if he please,
And feed on Stilton till he turns to cheese,

But cool Magendie proves beyond a doubt,
If mammals try it, that their eyes drop out.

No reasoning natures find it safe to feed,
For their sole diet, on a single creed;
It spoils their eyeballs while it spares their tongues,
And starves the heart to feed the noisy lungs.

When the first larvæ on the elm are seen,
The crawling wretches, like its leaves, are green;
Ere chill October shakes the latest down,
They, like the foliage, change their tint to brown;
On the blue flower a bluer flower you spy,
You stretch to pluck it — 't is a butterfly;
The flattened tree-toads so resemble bark,
They 're hard to find as Ethiops in the dark;
The woodcock, stiffening to fictitious mud,
Cheats the young sportsman thirsting for his blood.
So by long living on a single lie,
Nay, on one truth, will creatures get its dye;
Red, yellow, green, they take their subject's hue, —
Except when squabbling turns them black and blue

OUR LIMITATIONS.

We trust and fear, we question and believe,
From life's dark threads a trembling faith to weave,
Frail as the web that misty night has spun,
Whose dew-gemmed awnings glitter in the sun.
While the calm centuries spell their lessons out,
Each truth we conquer spreads the realm of doubt;
When Sinai's summit was Jehovah's throne,
The chosen Prophet knew his voice alone;
When Pilate's hall that awful question heard,
The Heavenly Captive answered not a word.

Eternal Truth! beyond our hopes and fears
Sweep the vast orbits of thy myriad spheres!
From age to age, while History carves sublime
On her waste rock the flaming curves of time,
How the wild swayings of our planet show
That worlds unseen surround the world we know!

THE OLD PLAYER.

The curtain rose; in thunders long and loud
The galleries rung; the veteran actor bowed.
In flaming line the telltales of the stage
Showed on his brow the autograph of age;
Pale, hueless waves amid his clustered hair,
And umbered shadows, prints of toil and care;
Round the wide circle glanced his vacant eye, —
He strove to speak, — his voice was but a sigh.

Year after year had seen its short-lived race
Flit past the scenes and others take their place;
Yet the old prompter watched his accents still,
His name still flaunted on the evening's bill.
Heroes, the monarchs of the scenic floor,
Had died in earnest and were heard no more;
Beauties, whose cheeks such roseate bloom o'erspread
They faced the footlights in unborrowed red,
Had faded slowly through successive shades
To gray duennas, foils of younger maids;
Sweet voices lost the melting tones that start
With Southern throbs the sturdy Saxon heart,
While fresh sopranos shook the painted sky

With their long, breathless, quivering locust-cry.
Yet there he stood, — the man of other days,
In the clear present's full, unsparing blaze,
As on the oak a faded leaf that clings
While a new April spreads its burnished wings.

How bright yon rows that soared in triple tier,
Their central sun the flashing chandelier!
How dim the eye that sought with doubtful aim
Some friendly smile it still might dare to claim!
How fresh these hearts! his own how worn and cold!
Such the sad thoughts that long-drawn sigh had told.

No word yet faltered on his trembling tongue;
Again, again, the crashing galleries rung.
As the old guardsman at the bugle's blast
Hears in its strain the echoes of the past;
So, as the plaudits rolled and thundered round,
A life of memories startled at the sound.

He lived again, — the page of earliest days, —
Days of small fee and parsimonious praise;
Then lithe young Romeo — hark that silvered tone,
From those smooth lips — alas! they were his own.
Then the bronzed Moor, with all his love and woe,
Told his strange tale of midnight melting snow;
And dark-plumed Hamlet, with his cloak and blade,
Looked on the royal ghost, himself a shade.

3 *

All in one flash, his youthful memories came,
Traced in bright hues of evanescent flame,
As the spent swimmer's in the lifelong dream,
While the last bubble rises through the stream.

Call him not old, whose visionary brain
Holds o'er the past its undivided reign.
For him in vain the envious seasons roll
Who bears eternal summer in his soul.
If yet the minstrel's song, the poet's lay,
Spring with her birds, or children at their play,
Or maiden's smile, or heavenly dream of art,
Stir the few life-drops creeping round his heart,
Turn to the record where his years are told, —
Count his gray hairs, — they cannot make him old!

What magic power has changed the faded mime?
One breath of memory on the dust of time.
As the last window in the buttressed wall
Of some gray minster tottering to its fall,
Though to the passing crowd its hues are spread,
A dull mosaic, yellow, green, and red,
Viewed from within, a radiant glory shows
When through its pictured screen the sunlight flows,
And kneeling pilgrims on its storied pane
See angels glow in every shapeless stain;

So streamed the vision through his sunken eye,
Clad in the splendors of his morning sky.

  All the wild hopes his eager boyhood knew,
All the young fancies riper years proved true,
The sweet, low-whispered words, the winning glance
From queens of song, from Houris of the dance,
Wealth's lavish gift, and Flattery's soothing phrase,
And Beauty's silence when her blush was praise,
And melting Pride, her lashes wet with tears,
Triumphs and banquets, wreaths and crowns and cheers,
Pangs of wild joy that perish on the tongue,
And all that poets dream, but leave unsung!

  In every heart some viewless founts are fed
From far-off hill-sides where the dews were shed;
On the worn features of the weariest face
Some youthful memory leaves its hidden trace,
As in old gardens left by exiled kings
The marble basins tell of hidden springs,
But, gray with dust, and overgrown with weeds,
Their choking jets the passer little heeds,
Till time's revenges break their seals away,
And, clad in rainbow light, the waters play.

  Good night, fond dreamer! let the curtain fall:
The world's a stage, and we are players all.

A strange rehearsal! Kings without their crowns,
And threadbare lords, and jewel-wearing clowns,
Speak the vain words that mock their throbbing hearts,
As Want, stern prompter! spells them out their parts.
The tinselled hero whom we praise and pay
Is twice an actor in a twofold play.
We smile at children when a painted screen
Seems to their simple eyes a real scene;
Ask the poor hireling, who has left his throne
To seek the cheerless home he calls his own,
Which of his double lives most real seems,
The world of solid fact or scenic dreams?
Canvas, or clouds, — the foot-lights, or the spheres, —
The play of two short hours, or seventy years?

  Dream on! Though Heaven may woo our open eyes,
Through their closed lids we look on fairer skies;
Truth is for other worlds, and hope for this;
The cheating future lends the present's bliss;
Life is a running shade, with fettered hands,
That chases phantoms over shifting sands;
Death a still spectre on a marble seat,
With ever clutching palms and shackled feet;
The airy shapes that mock life's slender chain,
The flying joys he strives to clasp in vain,
Death only grasps; to live is to pursue, —
Dream on! there's nothing but illusion true!

THE ISLAND RUIN.

Ye that have faced the billows and the spray
Of good St. Botolph's island-studded bay,
As from the gliding bark your eye has scanned
The beaconed rocks, the wave-girt hills of sand,
Have ye not marked one elm-o'ershadowed isle,
Round as the dimple chased in beauty's smile, —
A stain of verdure on an azure field,
Set like a jewel in a battered shield?
Fixed in the narrow gorge of Ocean's path,
Peaceful it meets him in his hour of wrath;
When the mailed Titan, scourged by hissing gales,
Writhes in his glistening coat of clashing scales;
The storm-beat island spreads its tranquil green,
Calm as an emerald on an angry queen.

  So fair when distant should be fairer near;
A boat shall waft us from the outstretched pier.
The breeze blows fresh; we reach the island's edge,
Our shallop rustling through the yielding sedge.

  No welcome greets us on the desert isle;
Those elms, far-shadowing, hide no stately pile:
Yet these green ridges mark an ancient road;
And lo! the traces of a fair abode;

The long gray line that marks a garden-wall,
And heaps of fallen beams, — fire-branded all.

  Who sees unmoved, a ruin at his feet,
The lowliest home where human hearts have beat?
Its hearth-stone, shaded with the bistre stain
A century's showery torrents wash in vain;
Its starving orchard, where the thistle blows
And mossy trunks still mark the broken rows;
Its chimney-loving poplar, oftenest seen
Next an old roof, or where a roof has been;
Its knot-grass, plantain, — all the social weeds,
Man's mute companions, following where he leads;
Its dwarfed, pale flowers, that show their straggling heads,
Sown by the wind from grass-choked garden-beds;
Its woodbine, creeping where it used to climb;
Its roses, breathing of the olden time;
All the poor shows the curious idler sees,
As life's thin shadows waste by slow degrees,
Till naught remains, the saddening tale to tell,
Save home's last wrecks, — the cellar and the well!

  And whose the home that strews in black decay
The one green-glowing island of the bay?
Some dark-browed pirate's, jealous of the fate
That seized the strangled wretch of "Nix's Mate"?

Some forger's, skulking in a borrowed name,
Whom Tyburn's dangling halter yet may claim?
Some wan-eyed exile's, wealth and sorrow's heir,
Who sought a lone retreat for tears and prayer?
Some brooding poet's, sure of deathless fame,
Had not his epic perished in the flame?
Or some gray wooer's, whom a girlish frown
Chased from his solid friends and sober town?
Or some plain tradesman's, fond of shade and ease,
Who sought them both beneath these quiet trees?
Why question mutes no question can unlock,
Dumb as the legend on the Dighton rock?
One thing at least these ruined heaps declare, —
They were a shelter once; a man lived there.

But where the charred and crumbling records fail,
Some breathing lips may piece the half-told tale;
No man may live with neighbors such as these,
Though girt with walls of rock and angry seas,
And shield his home, his children, or his wife,
His ways, his means, his vote, his creed, his life,
From the dread sovereignty of Ears and Eyes
And the small member that beneath them lies.

They told strange things of that mysterious man;
Believe who will, deny them such as can;
Why should we fret if every passing sail

Had its old seaman talking on the rail?
The deep-sunk schooner stuffed with Eastern lime,
Slow wedging on, as if the waves were slime;
The knife-edged clipper with her ruffled spars,
The pawing steamer with her mane of stars,
The bull-browed galliot butting through the stream,
The wide-sailed yacht that slipped along her beam,
The deck-piled sloops, the pinched chebacco-boats,
The frigate, black with thunder-freighted throats,
All had their talk about the lonely man;
And thus, in varying phrase, the story ran.

  His name had cost him little care to seek,
Plain, honest, brief, a decent name to speak,
Common, not vulgar, just the kind that slips
With least suggestion from a stranger's lips.
His birthplace England, as his speech might show,
Or his hale cheek, that wore the red-streak's glow;
His mouth sharp-moulded; in its mirth or scorn
There came a flash as from the milky corn,
When from the ear you rip the rustling sheath,
And the white ridges show their even teeth.
His stature moderate, but his strength confessed,
In spite of broadcloth, by his ample breast;
Full-armed, thick-handed; one that had been strong,
And might be dangerous still, if things went wrong.

He lived at ease beneath his elm-trees' shade,
Did naught for gain, yet all his debts were paid;
Rich, so 't was thought, but careful of his store;
Had all he needed, claimed to have no more.

But some that lingered round the isle at night
Spoke of strange stealthy doings in their sight;
Of creeping lonely visits that he made
To nooks and corners, with a torch and spade.
Some said they saw the hollow of a cave;
One, given to fables, swore it was a grave;
Whereat some shuddered, others boldly cried,
Those prowling boatmen lied, and knew they lied.

They said his house was framed with curious cares,
Lest some old friend might enter unawares;
That on the platform at his chamber's door
Hinged a loose square that opened through the floor;
Touch the black silken tassel next the bell,
Down, with a crash, the flapping trap-door fell;
Three stories deep the falling wretch would strike,
To writhe at leisure on a boarder's pike.

By day armed always; double-armed at night,
His tools lay round him; wake him such as might.
A carbine hung beside his India fan,
His hand could reach a Turkish ataghan;
Pistols, with quaint-carved stocks and barrels gilt,

E

Crossed a long dagger with a jewelled hilt;
A slashing cutlass stretched along the bed; —
All this was what those lying boatmen said.

  Then some were full of wondrous stories told
About old chests and cupboards full of gold;
Of the wedged ingots and the silver bars
That cost old pirates ugly sabre-scars;
How his laced wallet often would disgorge
The fresh-faced guinea of an English George,
Or sweated ducat, palmed by Jews of yore,
Or double Joe, or Portuguese moidore,
And how his finger wore a rubied ring
Fit for the white-necked play-girl of a king.
But these fine legends, told with staring eyes,
Met with small credence from the old and wise.

  Why tell each idle guess, each whisper vain?
Enough: the scorched and cindered beams remain.
He came, a silent pilgrim to the West,
Some old-world mystery throbbing in his breast;
Close to the thronging mart he dwelt alone;
He lived; he died. The rest is all unknown.

  Stranger, whose eyes the shadowy isle survey,
As the black steamer dashes through the bay,
Why ask his buried secret to divine?
He was thy brother; speak, and tell us thine!

THE BANKER'S DINNER.

The Banker's dinner is the stateliest feast
The town has heard of for a year, at least;
The sparry lustres shed their broadest blaze,
Damask and silver catch and spread the rays;
The florist's triumphs crown the daintier spoil
Won from the sea, the forest, or the soil;
The steaming hot-house yields its largest pines,
The sunless vaults unearth their oldest wines.
With one admiring look the scene survey,
And turn a moment from the bright display.

Of all the joys of earthly pride or power,
What gives most life, worth living, in an hour?
When Victory settles on the doubtful fight
And the last foeman wheels in panting flight,
No thrill like this is felt beneath the sun;
Life's sovereign moment is a battle won.
  But say what next? To shape a Senate's choice
By the strong magic of the master's voice;
To ride the stormy tempest of debate
That whirls the wavering fortunes of the state.
  Third in the list, the happy lover's prize
Is won by honeyed words from women's eyes.

If some would have it first instead of third,
So let it be, — I answer not a word.

 The fourth, — sweet readers, let the thoughtless half
Have its small shrug and inoffensive laugh;
Let the grave quarter wear its virtuous frown,
The stern half-quarter try to scowl us down;
But the last eighth, the choice and sifted few,
Will hear my words, and, pleased, confess them true.

 Among the great whom Heaven has made to shine,
How few have learned the art of arts, — to dine!
Nature, indulgent to our daily need,
Kind-hearted mother! taught us all to feed;
But the chief art, — how rarely Nature flings
This choicest gift among her social kings!
Say, man of truth, has life a brighter hour
Than waits the chosen guest who knows his power?
 He moves with ease, itself an angel charm, —
Lifts with light touch my lady's jewelled arm,
Slides to his seat, half leading and half led,
Smiling but quiet till the grace is said,
Then gently kindles, while by slow degrees
Creep softly out the little arts that please;
Bright looks, the cheerful language of the eye,
The neat, crisp question and the gay reply, —
Talk light and airy, such as well may pass

THE BANKER'S DINNER.

Between the rested fork and lifted glass; —
With play like this the earlier evening flies,
Till rustling silks proclaim the ladies rise.
 His hour has come, — he looks along the chairs,
As the Great Duke surveyed his iron squares.
— That's the young traveller, — is n't much to show,
Fast on the road, but at the table slow.
— Next him, — you see the author in his look, —
His forehead lined with wrinkles like a book, —
Wrote the great history of the ancient Huns, —
Holds back to fire among the heavy guns.
— O, there's our poet seated at his side,
Beloved of ladies, soft, cerulean-eyed.
Poets are prosy in their common talk,
As the fast trotters, for the most part, walk.
— And there's our well-dressed gentleman, who sits,
By right divine, no doubt, among the wits,
Who airs his tailor's patterns when he walks,
The man that often speaks, but never talks.
Why should he talk, whose presence lends a grace
To every table where he shows his face?
He knows the manual of the silver fork,
Can name his claret — if he sees the cork, —
Remark that "White-top" was considered fine,
But swear the "Juno" is the better wine; —

Is not this talking? Ask Quintilian's rules;
If they say No, the town has many fools.
— Pause for a moment, — for our eyes behold
The plain unsceptred king, the man of gold,
The thrice illustrious threefold millionnaire;
Mark his slow-creeping, dead, metallic stare;
His eyes, dull glimmering, like the balance-pan
That weighs its guinea as he weighs his man.
— Who's next? An artist, in a satin tie
Whose ample folds defeat the curious eye.
— And there's the cousin, — must be asked, you know, —
Looks like a spinster at a baby-show.
Hope he is cool, — they set him next the door, —
And likes his place, between the gap and bore.
— Next comes a Congress-man, distinguished guest!
We don't count him, — they asked him with the rest;
And then some white cravats, with well-shaped ties,
And heads above them which their owners prize.

Of all that cluster round the genial board,
Not one so radiant as the banquet's lord.
Some say they fancy, but they know not why,
A shade of trouble brooding in his eye,
Nothing, perhaps, — the rooms are over-hot, —
Yet see his cheek, — the dull-red burning spot, —

Taste the brown sherry which he does not pass, —
Ha! That is brandy; see him fill his glass!
  But not forgetful of his feasting friends,
To each in turn some lively word he sends;
See how he throws his baited lines about,
And plays his men as anglers play their trout.
  With the dry sticks all bonfires are begun;
Bring the first fagot, proser number one!
A question drops among the listening crew
And hits the traveller, pat on Timbuctoo.
We 're on the Niger, somewhere near its source, —
Not the least hurry, take the river's course
Through Kissi, Foota, Kankan, Bammakoo,
Bambarra, Sego, so to Timbuctoo,
Thence down to Youri; — stop him if we can,
We can't fare worse, — wake up the Congress-man!
The Congress-man, once on his talking legs,
Stirs up his knowledge to its thickest dregs.
Tremendous draught for dining men to quaff!
Nothing will choke him but a purpling laugh.
A word, — a shout, — a mighty roar, — 't is done;
Extinguished; lassoed by a treacherous pun.
  A laugh is priming to the loaded soul;
The scattering shots become a steady roll,
Broke by sharp cracks that run along the line,

The light artillery of the talker's wine.
The kindling goblets flame with golden dews,
The hoarded flasks their tawny fire diffuse,
And the Rhine's breast-milk gushes cold and bright,
Pale as the moon and maddening as her light;
With crimson juice the thirsty southern sky
Sucks from the hills where buried armies lie,
So that the dreamy passion it imparts
Is drawn from heroes' bones and lovers' hearts.

But lulls will come; the flashing soul transmits
Its gleams of light in alternating fits.
The shower of talk that rattled down amain
Ends in small patterings like an April's rain;
The voices halt; the game is at a stand;
Now for a solo from the master-hand!

'T is but a story, — quite a simple thing, —
An *aria* touched upon a single string,
But every accent comes with such a grace
The stupid servants listen in their place,
Each with his waiter in his lifted hands,
Still as a well-bred pointer when he stands.
A query checks him: "Is he quite exact?" —
(This from a grizzled, square-jawed man of fact.)
The sparkling story leaves him to his fate,
Crushed by a witness, smothered with a date,

As a swift river, sown with many a star,
Runs brighter, rippling on a shallow bar.
The smooth divine suggests a graver doubt;
A neat quotation bowls the parson out;
Then, sliding gayly from his own display,
He laughs the learned dulness all away.

  So, with the merry tale and jovial song,
The jocund evening whirls itself along,
Till the last chorus shrieks its loud *encore*,
And the white neckcloths vanish through the door.

  One savage word! — The menials know its tone,
And slink away; the master stands alone.
"Well played, by —"; breathe not what were best
    unheard;
His goblet shivers while he speaks the word, —
"If wine tells truth, — and so have said the wise, —
It makes me laugh to think how brandy lies!
Bankrupt to-morrow, — millionnaire to-day, —
The farce is over, — now begins the play!"

  The spring he touches lets a panel glide;
An iron closet lurks beneath the slide,
Bright with such treasures as a search might bring
From the deep pockets of a truant king.
Two diamonds, eyeballs of a God of bronze,

Bought from his faithful priest, a pious Bonze;
A string of brilliants; rubies, three or four;
Bags of old coin and bars of virgin ore;
A jewelled poniard and a Turkish knife,
Noiseless and useful if we come to strife.

 Gone! As a pirate flies before the wind,
And not one tear for all he leaves behind!
From all the love his better years have known
Fled like a felon, — ah! but not alone!
The chariot flashes through a lantern's glare, —
O the wild eyes! the storm of sable hair!
Still to his side the broken heart will cling, —
The bride of shame, — the wife without the ring:
Hark, the deep oath, — the wail of frenzied woe, —
Lost! lost to hope of Heaven and peace below!

 He kept his secret; but the seed of crime
Bursts of itself in God's appointed time.
The lives he wrecked were scattered far and wide;
One never blamed nor wept, — she only died.
None knew his lot, though idle tongues would say
He sought a lonely refuge far away,
And there, with borrowed name and altered mien,
He died unheeded, as he lived unseen.
The moral market had the usual chills

Of Virtue suffering from protested bills:
The White Cravats, to friendship's memory true,
Sighed for the past, surveyed the future too;
Their sorrow breathed in one expressive line, —
"Gave pleasant dinners; who has got his wine?"

THE MYSTERIOUS ILLNESS.

WHAT ailed young Lucius? Art had vainly tried
To guess his ill, and found herself defied.
The Augur plied his legendary skill;
Useless; the fair young Roman languished still.
His chariot took him every cloudless day
Along the Pincian Hill or Appian Way;
They rubbed his wasted limbs with sulphurous oil,
Oozed from the far-off Orient's heated soil;
They led him tottering down the steamy path
Where bubbling fountains filled the thermal bath;
Borne in his litter to Egeria's cave,
They washed him, shivering, in her icy wave.
They sought all curious herbs and costly stones,
They scraped the moss that grew on dead men's bones,
They tried all cures the votive tablets taught,
   Scoured every place whence healing drugs were
      brought,

O'er Thracian hills his breathless couriers ran,
His slaves waylaid the Syrian caravan.

  At last a servant heard a stranger speak
A new chirurgeon's name; a clever Greek,
Skilled in his art; from Pergamus he came
To Rome but lately; GALEN was the name.
The Greek was called: a man with piercing eyes,
Who must be cunning, and who might be wise.
He spoke but little, — if they pleased, he said,
He 'd wait awhile beside the sufferer's bed.
So by his side he sat, serene and calm,
His very accents soft as healing balm;
Not curious seemed, but every movement spied,
His sharp eyes searching where they seemed to glide;
Asked a few questions, — what he felt, and where?
"A pain just here," "A constant beating there."
Who ordered bathing for his aches and ails?
"Charmis, the water-doctor from Marseilles."
What was the last prescription in his case?
"A draught of wine with powdered chrysoprase."
Had he no secret grief he nursed alone?
A pause; a little tremor; answer, — "None."

  Thoughtful, a moment, sat the cunning leech,
And muttered "Eros!" in his native speech.

In the broad atrium various friends await
The last new utterance from the lips of fate;
Men, matrons, maids, they talk the question o'er,
And, restless, pace the tessellated floor.
Not unobserved the youth so long had pined,
By gentle-hearted dames and damsels kind;
One with the rest, a rich Patrician's pride,
The lady Hermia, called " the golden-eyed; "
The same the old Proconsul fain must woo,
Whom, one dark night, a masked sicarius slew;
The same black Crassus over roughly pressed
To hear his suit, — the Tiber knows the rest.
(Crassus was missed next morning by his set;
Next week the fishers found him in their net.)
She with the others paced the ample hall,
Fairest, alas! and saddest of them all.

At length the Greek declared, with puzzled face,
Some strange enchantment mingled in the case,
And naught would serve to act as counter-charm
Save a warm bracelet from a maiden's arm.
Not every maiden's, — many might be tried;
Which not in vain, experience must decide.
Were there no damsels willing to attend
And do such service for a suffering friend?

The message passed among the waiting crowd,

First in a whisper, then proclaimed aloud.
Some wore no jewels ; some were disinclined,
For reasons better guessed at than defined ;
Though all were saints, — at least professed to be, —
The list all counted, there were named but three.

   The leech, still seated by the patient's side,
Held his thin wrist, and watched him, eagle-eyed.
   Aurelia first, a fair-haired Tuscan girl,
Slipped off her golden asp, with eyes of pearl.
His solemn head the grave physician shook ;
The waxen features thanked her with a look.

   Olympia next, a creature half divine,
Sprung from the blood of old Evander's line,
Held her white arm, that wore a twisted chain
Clasped with an opal-sheeny cymophane.
In vain, O daughter ! said the baffled Greek.
The patient sighed the thanks he could not speak.

   Last, Hermia entered ; look, that sudden start !
The pallium heaves above his leaping heart ;
The beating pulse, the cheek's rekindled flame,
Those quivering lips, the secret all proclaim.
The deep disease long throbbing in the breast,
The dread enchantment, all at once confessed !
The case was plain ; the treatment was begun ;
And Love soon cured the mischief he had done.

Young Love, too oft thy treacherous bandage slips
Down from the eyes it blinded to the lips!
Ask not the Gods, O youth, for clearer sight,
But the bold heart to plead thy cause aright.
And thou, fair maiden, when thy lovers sigh,
Suspect thy flattering ear, but trust thine eye,
And learn this secret from the tale of old:
No love so true as love that dies untold.

A MOTHER'S SECRET.

How sweet the sacred legend — if unblamed
In my slight verse such holy things are named —
Of Mary's secret hours of hidden joy,
Silent, but pondering on her wondrous boy!
Ave, Maria! Pardon, if I wrong
Those heavenly words that shame my earthly song!

   The choral host had closed the Angels' strain
Sung to the listening watch on Bethlehem's plain,
And now the shepherds, hastening on their way,
Sought the still hamlet where the Infant lay.
They passed the fields that gleaning Ruth toiled o'er, —
They saw afar the ruined threshing-floor
Where Moab's daughter, homeless and forlorn,

Found Boaz slumbering by his heaps of corn;
And some remembered how the holy scribe,
Skilled in the lore of every jealous tribe,
Traced the warm blood of Jesse's royal son
To that fair alien, bravely wooed and won.
So fared they on to seek the promised sign
That marked the anointed heir of David's line.

 At last, by forms of earthly semblance led,
They found the crowded inn, the oxen's shed.
No pomp was there, no glory shone around
On the coarse straw that strewed the reeking ground;
One dim retreat a flickering torch betrayed, —
In that poor cell the Lord of Life was laid!

 The wondering shepherds told their breathless tale
Of the bright choir that woke the sleeping vale;
Told how the skies with sudden glory flamed,
Told how the shining multitude proclaimed
" Joy, joy to earth! Behold the hallowed morn!
In David's city Christ the Lord is born!
' Glory to God!' let angels shout on high,
' Good will to men!' the listening earth reply!"

 They spoke with hurried words and accents wild;
Calm in his cradle slept the heavenly child.
No trembling word the mother's joy revealed, —
One sigh of rapture, and her lips were sealed;

Unmoved she saw the rustic train depart,
But kept their words to ponder in her heart.

  Twelve years had passed; the boy was fair and tall,
Growing in wisdom, finding grace with all.
The maids of Nazareth, as they trooped to fill
Their balanced urns beside the mountain rill, —
The gathered matrons, as they sat and spun, —
Spoke in soft words of Joseph's quiet son.
No voice had reached the Galilean vale
Of star-led kings, or awe-struck shepherd's tale;
In the meek, studious child they only saw
The future Rabbi, learned in Israel's law.

  So grew the boy, and now the feast was near
When at the Holy Place the tribes appear.
Scarce had the home-bred child of Nazareth seen
Beyond the hills that girt the village green,
Save when at midnight, o'er the starlit sands,
Snatched from the steel of Herod's murdering bands,
A babe, close folded to his mother's breast,
Through Edom's wilds he sought the sheltering West.

  Then Joseph spake: "Thy boy hath largely grown;
Weave him fine raiment, fitting to be shown;
Fair robes beseem the pilgrim, as the priest:
Goes he not with us to the holy feast?"

And Mary culled the flaxen fibres white;
Till eve she spun; she spun till morning light.
The thread was twined; its parting meshes through
From hand to hand her restless shuttle flew,
Till the full web was wound upon the beam;
Love's curious toil, — a vest without a seam!

They reach the Holy Place, fulfil the days
To solemn feasting given, and grateful praise.
At last they turn, and far Moriah's height
Melts in the southern sky and fades from sight.
All day the dusky caravan has flowed
In devious trails along the winding road;
(For many a step their homeward path attends,
And all the sons of Abraham are as friends.)
Evening has come, — the hour of rest and joy, —
Hush! Hush! That whisper, — "Where is Mary's
    boy?"

O weary hour! O aching days that passed
Filled with strange fears each wilder than the last, —
The soldier's lance, the fierce centurion's sword,
The crushing wheels that whirl some Roman lord,
The midnight crypt that sucks the captive's breath,
The blistering sun on Hinnom's vale of death!

Thrice on his cheek had rained the morning light;
Thrice on his lips the mildewed kiss of night,

Crouched by a sheltering column's shining plinth,
Or stretched beneath the odorous terebinth.

  At last, in desperate mood, they sought once more
The Temple's porches, searched in vain before;
They found him seated with the ancient men, —
The grim old rufflers of the tongue and pen, —
Their bald heads glistening as they clustered near,
Their gray beards slanting as they turned to hear,
Lost in half-envious wonder and surprise
That lips so fresh should utter words so wise.

  And Mary said, — as one who, tried too long,
Tells all her grief and half her sense of wrong, —
"What is this thoughtless thing which thou hast
    done?
Lo, we have sought thee sorrowing, O my son!"

  Few words he spake, and scarce of filial tone,
Strange words, their sense a mystery yet unknown;
Then turned with them and left the holy hill,
To all their mild commands obedient still.

  The tale was told to Nazareth's sober men,
And Nazareth's matrons told it oft again,
The maids retold it at the fountain's side,
The youthful shepherds doubted or denied;
It passed around among the listening friends,
With all that fancy adds and fiction lends,

Till newer marvels dimmed the young renown
Of Joseph's son, who talked the Rabbis down.

But Mary, faithful to its lightest word,
Kept in her heart the sayings she had heard,
Till the dread morning rent the Temple's veil,
And shuddering earth confirmed the wondrous tale.

Youth fades; love droops; the leaves of friendship fall;
A mother's secret hope outlives them all.

THE DISAPPOINTED STATESMAN.

Who of all statesmen is his country's pride,
Her councils' prompter and her leaders' guide?
He speaks; the nation holds its breath to hear;
He nods, and shakes the sunset hemisphere.
Born where the primal fount of Nature springs
By the rude cradles of her throneless kings,
In his proud eye her royal signet flames,
By his own lips her Monarch she proclaims.

Why name his countless triumphs, whom to meet
Is to be famous, envied in defeat?
The keen debaters, trained to brawls and strife,
Who fire one shot, and finish with the knife,

Tried him but once, and, cowering in their shame,
Ground their hacked blades to strike at meaner game.
The lordly chief, his party's central stay,
Whose lightest word a hundred votes obey,
Found a new listener seated at his side,
Looked in his eye, and felt himself defied,
Flung his rash gauntlet on the startled floor,
Met the all-conquering, fought — and ruled no more.

  See where he moves, what eager crowds attend!
What shouts of thronging multitudes ascend!
If this is life, — to mark with every hour
The purple deepening in his robes of power,
To see the painted fruits of honor fall
Thick at his feet, and choose among them all,
To hear the sounds that shape his spreading name
Peal through the myriad organ-stops of fame,
Stamp the lone isle that spots the seaman's chart,
And crown the pillared glory of the mart,
To count as peers the few supremely wise
Who mark their planet in the angels' eyes, —
If this is life —

             What savage man is he
Who strides alone beside the sounding sea?
Alone he wanders by the murmuring shore,
His thoughts as restless as the waves that roar;

Looks on the sullen sky as stormy-browed
As on the waves yon tempest-brooding cloud,
Heaves from his aching breast a wailing sigh,
Sad as the gust that sweeps the clouded sky.

  Ask him his griefs; what midnight demons plough
The lines of torture on his lofty brow;
Unlock those marble lips and bid them speak
The mystery freezing in his bloodless cheek.

  His secret? Hid beneath a flimsy word;
One foolish whisper that ambition heard;
And thus it spake: "Behold yon gilded chair,
The world's one vacant throne, — thy place is there!

  Ah, fatal dream! What warning spectres meet
In ghastly circle round its shadowy seat!
Yet still the Tempter murmurs in his ear
The maddening taunt he cannot choose but hear:

"Meanest of slaves, by Gods and men accurst,
He who is second when he might be first!
Climb with bold front the ladder's topmost round,
Or chain thy creeping footsteps to the ground!"

  Illustrious Dupe! Have those majestic eyes
Lost their proud fire for such a vulgar prize?
Art thou the last of all mankind to know
That party-fights are won by aiming low?
Thou, stamped by Nature with her royal sign,

That party-hirelings hate a look like thine?
Shake from thy sense the wild delusive dream!
Without the purple, art thou not supreme?
And soothed by love unbought, thy heart shall own
A nation's homage nobler than its throne!

THE SECRET OF THE STARS.

Is man's the only throbbing heart that hides
The silent spring that feeds its whispering tides?
Speak from thy caverns, mystery-breeding Earth,
Tell the half-hinted story of thy birth,
And calm the noisy champions who have thrown
The book of types against the book of stone!

   Have ye not secrets, ye refulgent spheres,
No sleepless listener of the starlight hears?
In vain the sweeping equatorial pries
Through every world-sown corner of the skies,
To the far orb that so remotely strays
Our midnight darkness is its noonday blaze;
In vain the climbing soul of creeping man
Metes out the heavenly concave with a span,
Tracks into space the long-lost meteor's trail,

And weighs an unseen planet in the scale;
Still o'er their doubts the wan-eyed watchers sigh,
And Science lifts her still unanswered cry:
"Are all these worlds, that speed their circling flight,
Dumb, vacant, soulless, — bawbles of the night?
Warmed with God's smile and wafted by his breath,
To weave in ceaseless round the dance of Death?
Or rolls a sphere in each expanding zone,
Crowned with a life as varied as our own?"

MAKER of earth and stars! If thou hast taught
By what thy voice hath spoke, thy hand hath wrought,
By all that Science proves, or guesses true,
More than thy Poet dreamed, thy Prophet knew, —
The heavens still bow in darkness at thy feet,
And shadows veil thy cloud-pavilioned seat!
Not for ourselves we ask thee to reveal
One awful word beneath the future's seal;
What thou shalt tell us, grant us strength to bear;
What thou withholdest is thy single care.
Not for ourselves; the present clings too fast,
Moored to the mighty anchors of the past;
But when, with angry snap, some cable parts,
The sound re-echoing in our startled hearts, —
When, through the wall that clasps the harbor round,

THE SECRET OF THE STARS.

And shuts the raving ocean from its bound,
Shattered and rent by sacrilegious hands,
The first mad billow leaps upon the sands, —
Then to the Future's awful page we turn,
And what we question hardly dare to learn.

Still let us hope! for while we seem to tread
The time-worn pathway of the nations dead,
Though Sparta laughs at all our warlike deeds,
And buried Athens claims our stolen creeds,
Though Rome, a spectre on her broken throne,
Beholds our eagle and recalls her own,
Though England fling her pennons on the breeze
And reign before us Mistress of the seas, —
While calm-eyed History tracks us circling round
Fate's iron pillar where they all were bound,
She sees new beacons crowned with brighter flame
Than the old watch-fires, like, but not the same!
Still in our path a larger curve she finds,
The spiral widening as the chain unwinds!
No shameless haste shall spot with bandit-crime
Our destined empire snatched before its time.
Wait, — wait, undoubting, for the winds have caught
From our bold speech the heritage of thought;
No marble form that sculptured truth can wear
Vies with the image shaped in viewless air;

And thought unfettered grows through speech to deeds,
As the broad forest marches in its seeds.
What though we perish ere the day is won?
Enough to see its glorious work begun!
The thistle falls before a trampling clown,
But who can chain the flying thistle-down?
Wait while the fiery seeds of freedom fly,
The prairie blazes when the grass is dry!

What arms might ravish, leave to peaceful arts,
Wisdom and love shall win the roughest hearts;
So shall the angel who has closed for man
The blissful garden since his woes began
Swing wide the golden portals of the West,
And Eden's secret stand at length confessed!

TO GOVERNOR SWAIN.

Dear Governor, if my skiff might brave
The winds that lift the ocean wave,
The mountain stream that loops and swerves
Through my broad meadow's channelled curves
Should waft me on from bound to bound
To where the River weds the Sound,
The Sound should give me to the Sea,
That to the Bay, the Bay to Thee.

It may not be; too long the track
To follow down or struggle back.
The sun has set on fair Naushon
Long ere my western blaze is gone;
The ocean disk is rolling dark
In shadows round your swinging bark,
While yet the yellow sunset fills
The stream that scarfs my spruce-clad hills;

The day-star wakes your island deer
Long ere my barn-yard chanticleer;
Your mists are soaring in the blue
While mine are sparks of glittering dew.

It may not be; O would it might,
Could I live o'er that glowing night!
What golden hours would come to life,
What goodly feats of peaceful strife, —
Such jests, that, drained of every joke,
The very bank of language broke, —
Such deeds, that laughter nearly died
With stitches in his belted side;
While Time, caught fast in pleasure's chain,
His double goblet snapped in twain,
And stood with half in either hand, —
Both brimming full, — but not of sand!

It may not be; I strive in vain
To break my slender household chain, —
Three pairs of little clasping hands,
One voice, that whispers, not commands.
Even while my spirit flies away,
My gentle jailers murmur nay;
All shapes of elemental wrath

They raise along my threatened path;
The storm grows black, the waters rise,
The mountains mingle with the skies,
The mad tornado scoops the ground,
The midnight robber prowls around,—
Thus, kissing every limb they tie,
They draw a knot and heave a sigh,
Till, fairly netted in the toil,
My feet are rooted to the soil.
Only the soaring wish is free!—
And that, dear Governor, flies to thee!

PITTSFIELD, 1851.

TO AN ENGLISH FRIEND.

The seed that wasteful autumn cast
To waver on its stormy blast,
Long o'er the wintry desert tost,
Its living germ has never lost.
Dropped by the weary tempest's wing,
It feels the kindling ray of spring,
And, starting from its dream of death,
Pours on the air its perfumed breath.

So, parted by the rolling flood,
The love that springs from common blood
Needs but a single sunlit hour
Of mingling smiles to bud and flower;
Unharmed its slumbering life has flown,
From shore to shore, from zone to zone,
Where summer's falling roses stain
The tepid waves of Pontchartrain,

Or where the lichen creeps below
Katahdin's wreaths of whirling snow.

Though fiery sun and stiffening cold
May change the fair ancestral mould,
No winter chills, no summer drains
The life-blood drawn from English veins,
Still bearing wheresoe'er it flows
The love that with its fountain rose,
Unchanged by space, unwronged by time,
From age to age, from clime to clime!

1852.

VIGNETTES.

1853.

AFTER A LECTURE ON WORDSWORTH.

Come, spread your wings, as I spread mine,
    And leave the crowded hall
For where the eyes of twilight shine
    O'er evening's western wall.

These are the pleasant Berkshire hills,
    Each with its leafy crown;
Hark! from their sides a thousand rills
    Come singing sweetly down.

A thousand rills; they leap and shine,
    Strained through the shadowy nooks,
Till, clasped in many a gathering twine,
    They swell a hundred brooks.

AFTER A LECTURE ON WORDSWORTH.

A hundred brooks, and still they run
    With ripple, shade, and gleam,
Till, clustering all their braids in one,
    They flow a single stream.

A bracelet spun from mountain mist,
    A silvery sash unwound,
With ox-bow curve and sinuous twist
    It writhes to reach the Sound.

This is my bark, — a pigmy's ship;
    Beneath a child it rolls;
Fear not, — one body makes it dip,
    But not a thousand souls.

Float we the grassy banks between;
    Without an oar we glide;
The meadows, drest in living green,
    Unroll on either side.

— Come, take the book we love so well,
    And let us read and dream
We see whate'er its pages tell,
    And sail an English stream.

Up to the clouds the lark has sprung,
    Still trilling as he flies;
The linnet sings as there he sung;
    The unseen cuckoo cries,

And daisies strew the banks along,
    And yellow kingcups shine,
With cowslips, and a primrose throng,
    And humble celandine.

Ah foolish dream! when Nature nursed
    Her daughter in the West,
The fount was drained that opened first;
    She bared her other breast.

On the young planet's orient shore
    Her morning hand she tried;
Then turned the broad medallion o'er
    And stamped the sunset side.

Take what she gives, her pine's tall stem,
    Her elm with hanging spray;
She wears her mountain diadem
    Still in her own proud way.

Look on the forests' ancient kings,
    The hemlock's towering pride:
Yon trunk had thrice a hundred rings,
    And fell before it died.

Nor think that Nature saves her bloom
    And slights our grassy plain;
For us she wears her court costume, —
    Look on its broidered train;

The lily with the sprinkled dots,
    Brands of the noontide beam;
The cardinal, and the blood-red spots,
    Its double in the stream,

As if some wounded eagle's breast,
    Slow throbbing o'er the plain,
Had left its airy path impressed
    In drops of scarlet rain.

And hark! and hark! the woodland rings;
    There thrilled the thrush's soul;
And look! that flash of flamy wings, —
    The fire-plumed oriole!

Above, the hen-hawk swims and swoops,
    Flung from the bright, blue sky;
Below, the robin hops, and whoops
    His piercing, Indian cry.

Beauty runs virgin in the woods
    Robed in her rustic green,
And oft a longing thought intrudes,
    As if we might have seen

Her every finger's every joint
    Ringed with some golden line,
Poet whom Nature did anoint!
    Had our wild home been thine.

Yet think not so; Old England's blood
    Runs warm in English veins;
But wafted o'er the icy flood
    Its better life remains:

Our children know each wild-wood smell,
    The bayberry and the fern,
The man who does not know them well
    Is all too old to learn.

Be patient! On the breathing page
  Still pants our hurried past;
Pilgrim and soldier, saint and sage, —
  The poet comes the last!

Though still the lark-voiced matins ring
  The world has known so long;
The wood-thrush of the West shall sing
  Earth's last sweet even-song!

AFTER A LECTURE ON MOORE.

SHINE soft, ye trembling tears of light
  That strew the mourning skies;
Hushed in the silent dews of night
  The harp of Erin lies.

What though her thousand years have past
  Of poets, saints, and kings, —
Her echoes only hear the last
  That swept those golden strings.

Fling o'er his mound, ye star-lit bowers,
   The balmiest wreaths ye wear,
Whose breath has lent your earth-born flowers
   Heaven's own ambrosial air.

Breathe, bird of night, thy softest tone,
   By shadowy grove and rill;
Thy song will soothe us while we own
   That his was sweeter still.

Stay, pitying Time, thy foot for him
   Who gave thee swifter wings,
Nor let thine envious shadow dim
   The light his glory flings.

If in his cheek unholy blood
   Burned for one youthful hour,
'T was but the flushing of the bud
   That blooms a milk-white flower.

Take him, kind mother, to thy breast,
   Who loved thy smiles so well,
And spread thy mantle o'er his rest
   Of rose and asphodel.

AFTER A LECTURE ON MOORE.

— The bark has sailed the midnight sea,
   The sea without a shore,
That waved its parting sign to thee,
   "A health to thee, Tom Moore!"

And thine, long lingering on the strand,
   Its bright-hued streamers furled,
Was loosed by age, with trembling hand,
   To seek the silent world.

Not silent! no, the radiant stars
   Still singing as they shine,
Unheard through earth's imprisoning bars,
   Have voices sweet as thine.

Wake, then, in happier realms above
   The songs of bygone years,
Till angels learn those airs of love
   That ravished mortal ears!

AFTER A LECTURE ON KEATS.

" Purpureos spargam flores."

The wreath that star-crowned Shelley gave
Is lying on thy Roman grave,
Yet on its turf young April sets
Her store of slender violets;
Though all the Gods their garlands shower,
I too may bring one purple flower.
— Alas! what blossom shall I bring,
That opens in my Northern spring?
The garden beds have all run wild,
So trim when I was yet a child;
Flat plantains and unseemly stalks
Have crept across the gravel walks;
The vines are dead, long, long ago,
The almond buds no longer blow.
No more upon its mound I see
The azure, plume-bound fleur-de-lis;
Where once the tulips used to show,
In straggling tufts the pansies grow;
The grass has quenched my white-rayed gem,
The flowering " Star of Bethlehem,"

Though its long blade of glossy green
And pallid stripe may still be seen.
Nature, who treads her nobles down,
And gives their birthright to the clown,
Has sown her base-born weedy things
Above the garden's queens and kings.
— Yet one sweet flower of ancient race
Springs in the old familiar place.
When snows were melting down the vale,
And Earth unlaced her icy mail,
And March his stormy trumpet blew,
And tender green came peeping through,
I loved the earliest one to seek
That broke the soil with emerald beak,
And watch the trembling bells so blue
Spread on the column as it grew.
Meek child of earth! thou wilt not shame
The sweet, dead poet's holy name;
The God of music gave thee birth
Called from the crimson-spotted earth,
Where, sobbing his young life away,
His own fair Hyacinthus lay.
— The hyacinth my garden gave
Shall lie upon that Roman grave!

AFTER A LECTURE ON SHELLEY.

One broad, white sail in Spezzia's treacherous bay;
   On comes the blast; too daring bark, beware!
The cloud has clasped her; lo! it melts away;
   The wide, waste waters, but no sail is there.

Morning: a woman looking on the sea;
   Midnight: with lamps the long verandah burns;
Come, wandering sail, they watch, they burn for thee
   Suns come and go, alas! no bark returns.

And feet are thronging on the pebbly sands,
   And torches flaring in the weedy caves,
Where'er the waters lay with icy hands
   The shapes uplifted from their coral graves.

Vainly they seek; the idle quest is o'er;
   The coarse, dark women, with their hanging locks,
And lean, wild children gather from the shore
   To the black hovels bedded in the rocks.

But Love still prayed, with agonizing wail,
  "One, one last look, ye heaving waters, yield!"
Till Ocean, clashing in his jointed mail,
  Raised the pale burden on his level shield.

Slow from the shore the sullen waves retire;
  His form a nobler element shall claim;
Nature baptized him in ethereal fire,
  And Death shall crown him with a wreath of flame.

Fade, mortal semblance, never to return;
  Swift is the change within thy crimson shroud;
Seal the white ashes in the peaceful urn;
  All else has risen in yon silvery cloud.

Sleep where thy gentle Adonais lies,
  Whose open page lay on thy dying heart,
Both in the smile of those blue-vaulted skies,
  Earth's fairest dome of all divinest art.

Breathe for his wandering soul one passing sigh,
  O happier Christian, while thine eye grows dim, —
In all the mansions of the house on high,
  Say not that Mercy has not one for him!

AT THE CLOSE OF A COURSE OF LECTURES.

As the voice of the watch to the mariner's dream ;
As the footstep of Spring on the ice-girdled stream,
There comes a soft footstep, a whisper, to me, —
The vision is over, — the rivulet free !

We have trod from the threshold of turbulent March,
Till the green scarf of April is hung on the larch,
And down the bright hill-side that welcomes the day,
We hear the warm panting of beautiful May.

We will part before Summer has opened her wing,
And the bosom of June swells the bodice of Spring,
While the hope of the season lies fresh in the bud,
And the young life of Nature runs warm in our blood.

It is but a word, and the chain is unbound,
The bracelet of steel drops unclasped to the ground ;
No hand shall replace it, — it rests where it fell, —
It is but one word that we all know too well.

Yet the hawk with the wildness untamed in his eye,
If you free him, stares round ere he springs to the sky;
The slave whom no longer his fetters restrain
Will turn for a moment and look at his chain.

Our parting is not as the friendship of years,
That chokes with the blessing it speaks through its tears;
We have walked in a garden, and, looking around,
Have plucked a few leaves from the myrtles we found.

But now at the gate of the garden we stand,
And the moment has come for unclasping the hand;
Will you drop it like lead, and in silence retreat
Like the twenty crushed forms from an omnibus seat?

Nay! hold it one moment, — the last we may share, —
I stretch it in kindness, and not for my fare;
You may pass through the doorway in rank or in file,
If your ticket from Nature is stamped with a smile.

For the sweetest of smiles is the smile as we part,
When the light round the lips is a ray from the heart;
And lest a stray tear from its fountain might swell,
We will seal the bright spring with a quiet farewell.

THE HUDSON.

AFTER A LECTURE AT ALBANY.

'T was a vision of childhood that came with its dawn,
Ere the curtain that covered life's day-star was drawn;
The nurse told the tale when the shadows grew long,
And the mother's soft lullaby breathed it in song.

"There flows a fair stream by the hills of the west," —
She sang to her boy as he lay on her breast;
"Along its smooth margin thy fathers have played;
Beside its deep waters their ashes are laid."

I wandered afar from the land of my birth,
I saw the old rivers, renowned upon earth,
But fancy still painted that wide-flowing stream
With the many-hued pencil of infancy's dream.

I saw the green banks of the castle-crowned Rhine,
Where the grapes drink the moonlight and change it to wine;
I stood by the Avon, whose waves as they glide
Still whisper his glory who sleeps at their side.

But my heart would still yearn for the sound of the
    waves
That sing as they flow by my forefathers' graves;
If manhood yet honors my cheek with a tear,
I care not who sees it, — no blush for it here!

Farewell to the deep-bosomed stream of the West!
I fling this loose blossom to float on its breast;
Nor let the dear love of its children grow cold,
Till the channel is dry where its waters have rolled!

DECEMBER, 1854.

A POEM

FOR THE MEETING OF THE AMERICAN MEDICAL ASSOCIATION

AT NEW YORK, MAY 5, 1853.

I HOLD a letter in my hand, —
  A flattering letter — more's the pity, —
By some contriving junto planned,
  And signed *per order of Committee;*
It touches every tenderest spot, —
  My patriotic predilections,
My well known — something — don't ask what,
  My poor old songs, my kind affections.

They make a feast on Thursday next,
  And hope to make the feasters merry;
They own they're something more perplexed
  For poets than for port and sherry; —
They want the men of — (word torn out);
  Our friends will come with anxious faces

(To see our blankets off, no doubt,
    And trot us out and show our paces).

They hint that papers by the score
    Are rather musty kind of rations;
They don't exactly mean a bore,
    But only trying to the patience;
That such as — you know who I mean —
    Distinguished for their — what d' ye call 'em —
Should bring the dews of Hippocrene
    To sprinkle on the faces solemn.

— The same old story; that's the chaff
    To catch the birds that sing the ditties;
Upon my soul, it makes me laugh
    To read these letters from Committees!
They're all *so* loving and *so* fair, —
    All for *your* sake such kind compunction, —
'T would save your carriage half its wear
    To touch its wheels with such an unction!

Why, who am I, to lift me here
    And beg such learned folk to listen, —
To ask a smile, or coax a tear
    Beneath these stoic lids to glisten?

As well might some arterial thread
    Ask the whole frame to feel it gushing,
While throbbing fierce from heel to head
    The vast aortic tide was rushing.

As well some hair-like nerve might strain
    To set its special streamlet going,
While through the myriad-channelled brain
    The burning flood of thought was flowing;
Or trembling fibre strive to keep
    The springing haunches gathered shorter,
While the scourged racer, leap on leap,
    Was stretching through the last hot quarter!

Ah me! you take the bud that came
    Self-sown in your poor garden's borders,
And hand it to the stately dame
    That florists breed for, all she orders;
She thanks you — it was kindly meant —
    (A pale affair, not worth the keeping,) —
Good morning; — and your bud is sent
    To join the tea-leaves used for sweeping.

Not always so, kind hearts and true, —
    For such I know are round me beating;

Is not the bud I offer you, —
  Fresh gathered for the hour of meeting, —
Pale though its outer leaves may be,
  Rose-red in all its inner petals,
Where the warm life we cannot see —
  The life of love that gave it — settles?

We meet from regions far away,
  Like rills from distant mountains streaming;
The sun is on Francisco's bay
  O'er Chesapeake the lighthouse gleaming;
While summer girds the still bayou
  In chains of bloom, her bridal token,
Monadnock sees the sky grow blue,
  His crystal bracelet yet unbroken.

Yet Nature bears the self-same heart
  Beneath her russet-mantled bosom,
As where with burning lips apart
  She breathes, and white magnolias blossom;
The self-same founts her chalice fill
  With showery sunlight running over,
On fiery plain and frozen hill,
  On myrtle-beds and fields of clover.

I give you *Home!* its crossing lines
    United in one golden suture,
And showing every day that shines
    The present growing to the future, —
A flag that bears a hundred stars,
    In one bright ring, with love for centre,
Fenced round with white and crimson bars,
    No prowling treason dares to enter!

O brothers, home may be a word
    To make affection's living treasure —
The wave an angel might have stirred —
    A stagnant pool of selfish pleasure;
HOME! It is where the day-star springs
    And where the evening sun reposes,
Where'er the eagle spreads his wings,
    From northern pines to southern roses!

THE NEW EDEN.

(MEETING OF THE BERKSHIRE HORTICULTURAL SOCIETY, AT STOCKBRIDGE, SEPT. 13, 1854.)

SCARCE could the parting ocean close,
    Seamed by the Mayflower's cleaving bow,
When o'er the rugged desert rose
    The waves that tracked the Pilgrim's plough.

Then sprang from many a rock-strewn field
    The rippling grass, the nodding grain,
Such growths as English meadows yield
    To scanty sun and frequent rain.

But when the fiery days were done,
    And Autumn brought his purple haze,
Then, kindling in the slanted sun,
    The hill-sides gleamed with golden maize.

The food was scant, the fruits were few:
    A red-streak glistened here and there;
Perchance in statelier precincts grew
    Some stern old Puritanic pear.

Austere in taste, and tough at core,
    Its unrelenting bulk was shed,
To ripen in the Pilgrim's store
    When all the summer sweets were fled.

Such was his lot, to front the storm
    With iron heart and marble brow,
Nor ripen till his earthly form
    Was cast from life's autumnal bough.

— But ever on the bleakest rock
    We bid the brightest beacon glow,
And still upon the thorniest stock
    The sweetest roses love to blow.

So on our rude and wintry soil
    We feed the kindling flame of art,
And steal the tropic's blushing spoil
    To bloom on Nature's ice-clad heart.

See how the softening Mother's breast
　　Warms to her children's patient wiles,—
Her lips by loving Labor pressed
　　Break in a thousand dimpling smiles,

From when the flushing bud of June
　　Dawns with its first auroral hue,
Till shines the rounded harvest-moon,
　　And velvet dahlias drink the dew.

Nor these the only gifts she brings;
　　Look where the laboring orchard groans,
And yields its beryl-threaded strings
　　For chestnut burs and hemlock cones.

Dear though the shadowy maple be,
　　And dearer still the whispering pine,
Dearest yon russet-laden tree
　　Browned by the heavy rubbing kine!

There childhood flung its rustling stone,
　　There venturous boyhood learned to climb,—
How well the early graft was known
　　Whose fruit was ripe ere harvest time!

Nor be the Fleming's pride forgot,
  With swinging drops and drooping bells,
Freckled and splashed with streak and spot,
  On the warm-breasted, sloping swells;

Nor Persia's painted garden-queen, —
  Frail Houri of the trellised wall, —
Her deep-cleft bosom scarfed with green, —
  Fairest to see, and first to fall.

— When man provoked his mortal doom,
  And Eden trembled as he fell,
When blossoms sighed their last perfume,
  And branches waved their long farewell,

One sucker crept beneath the gate,
  One seed was wafted o'er the wall,
One bough sustained his trembling weight;
  These left the garden, — these were all.

And far o'er many a distant zone
  These wrecks of Eden still are flung:
The fruits that Paradise hath known
  Are still in earthly gardens hung.

Yes, by our own unstoried stream
   The pink-white apple-blossoms burst
That saw the young Euphrates gleam, —
   That Gihon's circling waters nursed.

For us the ambrosial pear displays
   The wealth its arching branches hold,
Bathed by a hundred summery days
   In floods of mingling fire and gold.

And here, where beauty's cheek of flame
   With morning's earliest beam is fed,
The sunset-painted peach may claim
   To rival its celestial red.

— What though in some unmoistened vale
   The summer leaf grow brown and sere,
Say, shall our star of promise fail
   That circles half the rolling sphere,

From beaches salt with bitter spray,
   O'er prairies green with softest rain,
And ridges bright with evening's ray,
   To rocks that shade the stormless main?

If by our slender-threaded streams
   The blade and leaf and blossom die,
If, drained by noontide's parching beams,
   The milky veins of Nature dry,

See, with her swelling bosom bare,
   Yon wild-eyed Sister in the West, —
The ring of Empire round her hair,
   The Indian's wampum on her breast!

We saw the August sun descend,
   Day after day, with blood-red stain,
And the blue mountains dimly blend
   With smoke-wreaths from the burning plain;

Beneath the hot Sirocco's wings
   We sat and told the withering hours,
Till Heaven unsealed its hoarded springs,
   And bade them leap in flashing showers.

Yet in our Ishmael's thirst we knew
   The mercy of the Sovereign hand
Would pour the fountain's quickening dew
   To feed some harvest of the land.

No flaming swords of wrath surround
   Our second Garden of the Blest;
It spreads beyond its rocky bound,
   It climbs Nevada's glittering crest.

God keep the tempter from its gate!
   God shield the children, lest they fall
From their stern fathers' free estate, —
   Till Ocean is its only wall!

A SENTIMENT.

A TRIPLE health to Friendship, Science, Art,
From heads and hands that own a common heart!
Each in its turn the others' willing slave, —
Each in its season strong to heal and save.

Friendship's blind service, in the hour of need,
Wipes the pale face — and lets the victim bleed.
Science must stop to reason and explain;
ART claps his finger on the streaming vein.

But Art's brief memory fails the hand at last;
Then SCIENCE lifts the flambeau of the past.
When both their equal impotence deplore, —
When Learning sighs, and Skill can do no more, —
The tear of FRIENDSHIP pours its heavenly balm,
And soothes the pang no anodyne may calm!

May 1st, 1855.

SEMICENTENNIAL CELEBRATION OF THE NEW ENGLAND SOCIETY,

NEW YORK, DEC. 22, 1855.

New England, we love thee; no time can erase
From the hearts of thy children the smile on thy face.
'T is the mother's fond look of affection and pride,
As she gives her fair son to the arms of his bride.

His bride may be fresher in beauty's young flower;
She may blaze in the jewels she brings with her dower.
But passion must chill in Time's pitiless blast;
The one that first loved us will love to the last.

You have left the dear land of the lake and the hill,
But its winds and its waters will talk with you still.
"Forget not," they whisper, "your love is our debt,"
And echo breathes softly, " We never forget."

The banquet's gay splendors are gleaming around,
But your hearts have flown back o'er the waves of the
  Sound;
They have found the brown home where their pulses
  were born;
They are throbbing their way through the trees and the
  corn.

There are roofs you remember, — their glory is fled;
There are mounds in the churchyard, — one sigh for the
  dead.
There are wrecks, there are ruins, all scattered around;
But Earth has no spot like that corner of ground.

Come, let us be cheerful, — remember last night,
How they cheered us, and — never mind — meant it
  all right;
To-night, we harm nothing, — we love in the lump;
Here's a bumper to Maine, in the juice of the pump!

Here's to all the good people, wherever they be,
Who have grown in the shade of the liberty-tree;
We all love its leaves, and its blossoms and fruit,
But pray have a care of the fence round its root.

We should like to talk big; it's a kind of a right,
When the tongue has got loose and the waistband grown
    tight;
But, as pretty Miss Prudence remarked to her beau,
On its own heap of compost, no biddy should crow.

Enough! There are gentlemen waiting to talk,
Whose words are to mine as the flower to the stalk.
Stand by your old mother whatever befall;
God bless all her children! Good night to you all!

ODE FOR WASHINGTON'S BIRTHDAY.

**CELEBRATION OF THE MERCANTILE LIBRARY ASSOCIATION.
FEBRUARY 22, 1856.**

Welcome to the day returning,
   Dearer still as ages flow,
While the torch of Faith is burning,
   Long as Freedom's altars glow!
See the hero whom it gave us
   Slumbering on a mother's breast;
For the arm he stretched to save us,
   Be its morn forever blest!

Hear the tale of youthful glory,
   While of Britain's rescued band
Friend and foe repeat the story,
   Spread his fame o'er sea and land,
Where the red cross proudly streaming,
   Flaps above the frigate's deck,

Where the golden lilies, gleaming,
    Star the watch-towers of Quebec.

Look! The shadow on the dial
    Marks the hour of deadlier strife;
Days of terror, years of trial,
    Scourge a nation into life.
Lo, the youth, become her leader!
    All her baffled tyrants yield;
Through his arm the Lord hath freed her;
    Crown him on the tented field!

Vain is Empire's mad temptation;
    Not for him an earthly crown!
He whose sword hath freed a nation
    Strikes the offered sceptre down.
See the throneless Conqueror seated,
    Ruler by a people's choice;
See the Patriot's task completed;
    Hear the Father's dying voice!

"By the name that you inherit,
    By the sufferings you recall,
Cherish the fraternal spirit;
    Love your country first of all!

Listen not to idle questions
   If its bands may be untied;
Doubt the patriot whose suggestions
   Strive a nation to divide!"

Father! We, whose ears have tingled
   With the discord-notes of shame, —
We, whose sires their blood have mingled
   In the battle's thunder-flame, —
Gathering, while this holy morning
   Lights the land from sea to sea,
Hear thy counsel, heed thy warning;
   Trust us, while we honor thee!

CLASS OF '29.

FOR THURSDAY, NOVEMBER 6, 1856.

You'll believe me, dear boys, 't is a pleasure to rise
With a welcome like this in your darling old eyes,
To meet the same smiles and to hear the same tone
Which have greeted me oft in the years that have flown.

Were I gray as the grayest old rat in the wall,
My locks would turn brown at the sight of you all;
If my heart were as dry as the shell on the sand,
It would fill like the goblet I hold in my hand.

There are noontides of autumn, when summer returns,
Though the leaves are all garnered and sealed in their urns,
And the bird on his perch that was silent so long
Believes the sweet sunshine and breaks into song.

We have caged the young birds of our beautiful June:
Their plumes are still bright and their voices in tune;
One moment of sunshine from faces like these,
And they sing as they sung in the green-growing trees.

The voices of morning! How sweet is their thrill
When the shadows have turned, and the evening grows
    still!
The text of our lives may get wiser with age,
But the print was so fair on its twentieth page!

Look off from your goblet and up from your plate,
Come, take the last journal and glance at its date, —
Then think what we fellows should say and should do,
If the 6 were a 9, and the 5 were a 2.

Ah no! For the shapes that would meet with us here
From the far land of shadows are ever too dear!
Though youth flung around us its pride and its charms,
We should see but the comrades we clasped in our arms.

A health to our future, — a sigh for our past!
We love, we remember, we hope to the last;
And for all the base lies that the almanacs hold,
While we 've youth in our hearts, we can never grow
    old.

FOR THE MEETING OF THE BURNS CLUB.

1856.

THE mountains glitter in the snow
    A thousand leagues asunder;
Yet here, amid the banquet's glow,
    I hear their voice of thunder;
Each giant's ice-bound goblet clinks;
    A flowing stream is summoned;
Wachusett to Ben Nevis drinks;
    Monadnock to Ben Lomond!

Though years have clipped the eagle's plume
    That crowned the chieftain's bonnet,
The sun still sees the heather bloom,
    The silver mists lie on it;
With tartan kilt and philibeg,
    What stride was ever bolder
Than his who showed the naked leg
    Beneath the plaided shoulder?

The echoes sleep on Cheviot's hills,
    That heard the bugles blowing
When down their sides the crimson rills
    With mingled blood were flowing;
The hunts where gallant hearts were game,
    The slashing on the border,
The raid that swooped with sword and flame,
    Give place to "law and order."

Not while the rocking steeples reel
    With midnight tocsins ringing,
Not while the crashing war-notes peal,
    God sets his poets singing;
The bird is silent in the night,
    Or shrieks a cry of warning
While fluttering round the beacon-light, —
    But hear him greet the morning!

The lark of Scotia's morning sky!
    Whose voice may sing his praises?
With Heaven's own sunlight in his eye,
    He walked among the daisies,
Till through the cloud of fortune's wrong
    He soared to fields of glory;
But left his land her sweetest song
    And earth her saddest story.

'T is not the forts the builder piles
  That chain the earth together;
The wedded crowns, the sister isles,
  Would laugh at such a tether;
The kindling thought, the throbbing words,
  That set the pulses beating,
Are stronger than the myriad swords
  Of mighty armies meeting.

Thus while within the banquet glows,
  Without, the wild winds whistle,
We drink a triple health, — the Rose,
  The Shamrock, and the Thistle!
Their blended hues shall never fade
  Till War has hushed his cannon, —
Close-twined as ocean-currents braid
  The Thames, the Clyde, the Shannon!

FOR THE BURNS CENTENNIAL CELEBRATION.

JANUARY 25, 1859.

His birthday. — Nay, we need not speak
   The name each heart is beating, —
Each glistening eye and flushing cheek
   In light and flame repeating!

We come in one tumultuous tide, —
   One surge of wild emotion, —
As crowding through the Frith of Clyde
   Rolls in the Western Ocean;

As when yon cloudless, quartered moon
   Hangs o'er each storied river,
The swelling breasts of Ayr and Doon
   With sea-green wavelets quiver.

The century shrivels like a scroll, —
  The past becomes the present, —
And face to face, and soul to soul,
  We greet the monarch-peasant.

While Shenstone strained in feeble flights
  With Corydon and Phillis, —
While Wolfe was climbing Abraham's heights
  To snatch the Bourbon lilies, —

Who heard the wailing infant's cry,
  The babe beneath the shieling,
Whose song to-night in every sky
  Will shake earth's starry ceiling, —

Whose passion-breathing voice ascends
  And floats like incense o'er us,
Whose ringing lay of friendship blends
  With labor's anvil chorus?

We love him, not for sweetest song,
  Though never tone so tender;
We love him, even in his wrong, —
  His wasteful self-surrender.

We praise him, not for gifts divine, —
    His Muse was born of woman, —
His manhood breathes in every line, —
    Was ever heart more human?

We love him, praise him, just for this:
    In every form and feature,
Through wealth and want, through woe and bliss,
    He saw his fellow-creature!

No soul could sink beneath his love, —
    Not even angel blasted;
No mortal power could soar above
    The pride that all outlasted!

Ay! Heaven had set one living man
    Beyond the pedant's tether, —
His virtues, frailties, HE may scan,
    Who weighs them all together!

I fling my pebble on the cairn
    Of him, though dead, undying;
Sweet Nature's nursling, bonniest bairn
    Beneath her daisies lying.

The waning suns, the wasting globe,
   Shall spare the minstrel's story, —
The centuries weave his purple robe,
   The mountain-mist of glory!

BIRTHDAY OF DANIEL WEBSTER.

January 18, 1856.

When life hath run its largest round
   Of toil and triumph, joy and woe,
How brief a storied page is found
   To compass all its outward show!

The world-tried sailor tires and droops;
   His flag is rent, his keel forgot;
His farthest voyages seem but loops
   That float from life's entangled knot.

But when within the narrow space
   Some larger soul hath lived and wrought,
Whose sight was open to embrace
   The boundless realms of deed and thought,—

When, stricken by the freezing blast,
    A nation's living pillars fall,
How rich the storied page, how vast,
    A word, a whisper can recall!

No medal lifts its fretted face,
    Nor speaking marble cheats your eye,
Yet, while these pictured lines I trace,
    A living image passes by:

A roof beneath the mountain pines;
    The cloisters of a hill-girt plain;
The front of life's embattled lines;
    A mound beside the heaving main.

These are the scenes: a boy appears;
    Set life's round dial in the sun,
Count the swift arc of seventy years,
    His frame is dust; his task is done.

Yet pause upon the noontide hour,
    Ere the declining sun has laid
His bleaching rays on manhood's power,
    And look upon the mighty shade.

No gloom that stately shape can hide,
    No change uncrown its brow; behold!
Dark, calm, large-fronted, lightning-eyed,
    Earth has no double from its mould!

Ere from the fields by valor won
    The battle-smoke had rolled away,
And bared the blood-red setting sun,
    His eyes were opened on the day.

His land was but a shelving strip
    Black with the strife that made it free;
He lived to see its banners dip
    Their fringes in the Western sea.

The boundless prairies learned his name,
    His words the mountain echoes knew,
The Northern breezes swept his fame
    From icy lake to warm bayou.

In toil he lived; in peace he died;
    When life's full cycle was complete,
Put off his robes of power and pride,
    And laid them at his Master's feet.

His rest is by the storm-swept waves
    Whom life's wild tempests roughly tried,
Whose heart was like the streaming caves
    Of ocean, throbbing at his side.

Death's cold white hand is like the snow
    Laid softly on the furrowed hill,
It hides the broken seams below,
    And leaves the summit brighter still.

In vain the envious tongue upbraids;
    His name a nation's heart shall keep
Till morning's latest sunlight fades
    On the blue tablet of the deep!

MEETING OF THE ALUMNI OF HARVARD COLLEGE.

1857.

I THANK you, MR. PRESIDENT, you've kindly broke the ice;
Virtue should always be the first, — I'm only SECOND VICE —
(A vice is something with a screw that's made to hold its jaw
Till some old file has played away upon an ancient saw.)

Sweet brothers by the Mother's side, the babes of days gone by,
All nurslings of her Juno breasts whose milk is never dry,

We come again, like half-grown boys, and gather at her
    beck
About her knees, and on her lap, and clinging round
    her neck.

We find her at her stately door, and in her ancient chair,
Dressed in the robes of red and green she always loved
    to wear.
Her eye has all its radiant youth, her cheek its morning
    flame;
We drop our roses as we go, hers flourish still the same.

We have been playing many an hour, and far away
    we've strayed,
Some laughing in the cheerful sun, some lingering in
    the shade;
And some have tired, and laid them down where darker
    shadows fall, —
Dear as her loving voice may be, they cannot hear its
    call.

What miles we've travelled since we shook the dew-
    drops from our shoes
We gathered on this classic green, so famed for heavy
    dues!

How many boys have joined the game, how many
    slipped away,
Since we've been running up and down, and having
    out our play!

One boy at work with book and brief, and one with
    gown and band,
One sailing vessels on the pool, one digging in the sand,
One flying paper kites on change, one planting little
    pills, —
The seeds of certain annual flowers well known as little
    bills.

What maidens met us on our way, and clasped us hand
    in hand!
What cherubs, — not the legless kind, that fly, but
    never stand!
How many a youthful head we've seen put on its silver
    crown!
What sudden changes back again to youth's empurpled
    brown!

But fairer sights have met our eyes, and broader lights
    have shone,
Since others lit their midnight lamps where once we
    trimmed our own;

A thousand **trains** that flap the sky with flags **of** rushing fire,
And, throbbing in the Thunderer's **hand, Thought's**
million-chorded **lyre.**

We've seen the sparks of Empire fly beyond the mountain bars,
Till, glittering o'er the Western wave, they joined **the**
setting stars;
And ocean trodden into paths that trampling **giants**
ford,
To **find the** planet's **vertebræ** and sink its spinal **cord.**

We **'ve** tried reform, — and chloroform, — and both
have turned our brain;
When France called up the photograph, we roused the
foe to pain;
Just so those earlier sages shared the chaplet **of** renown, —
Hers sent a **bladder to** the clouds, ours brought their
lightning down.

We've **seen the** little tricks of life, its varnish and
veneer,
Its stucco-fronts of character flake off and disappear;

We've learned that oft the brownest hands will heap
   the biggest pile,
And met with many a "perfect brick" beneath a rim-
   less " tile."

What dreams we've had of deathless name, as scholars,
   statesmen, bards,
While Fame, the lady with the trump, held up her picture cards!
Till, having nearly played our game, she gayly whispered, "Ah!
I said you should be something grand, — you'll soon
   be grandpapa."

Well, well, the old have had their day, the young must
   take their turn ;
There's something always to forget, and something still
   to learn ;
But how to tell what's old or young, the tap-root from
   the sprigs,
Since Florida revealed her fount to Ponce de Leon
   Twiggs?

The wisest was a Freshman once, just freed from bar
   and bolt,
As noisy as a kettle-drum, as leggy as a colt ;

Don't be too savage with the boys, — the Primer does
    not say
The kitten ought to go to church because "the cat doth
    prey."

The law of merit and of age is not the rule of three;
Non constat that A. M. must prove as busy as A. B.
When Wise the father tracked the son, ballooning
    through the skies,
He taught a lesson to the old, — go thou and do like
    Wise!

Now then, old boys, and reverend youth, of high or low
    degree,
Remember how we only get one annual out of three,
And such as dare to simmer down three dinners into
    one
Must cut their salads mighty short, and pepper well
    with fun.

I've passed my zenith long ago, it's time for me to set;
A dozen planets wait to shine, and I am lingering yet,
As sometimes in the blaze of day a milk-and-watery
    moon
Stains with its dim and fading ray the lustrous blue of
    noon.

Farewell! yet let one echo rise to shake our ancient hall;
God save the Queen, — whose throne is here, — the Mother of us all!
Till dawns the great Commencement-day on every shore and sea,
And "Expectantur" all mankind, to take their last Degree!

THE PARTING SONG.

FESTIVAL OF THE ALUMNI, 1857.

The noon of summer sheds its ray
  On Harvard's holy ground;
The Matron calls, the sons obey,
  And gather smiling round.

CHORUS. — Then old and young together stand,
    The sunshine and the snow,
  As heart to heart and hand in hand,
    We sing before we go!

Her hundred opening doors have swung;
  Through every storied hall
The pealing echoes loud have rung,
  "Thrice welcome one and all!"
    Then old and young, etc.

We floated through her peaceful bay,
    To sail life's stormy seas;
But left our anchor where it lay
    Beneath her green old trees.
        Then old and young, etc.

As now we lift its lengthening chain,
    That held us fast of old,
The rusted rings grow bright again, —
    Their iron turns to gold.
        Then old and young, etc.

Though scattered ere the setting sun,
    As leaves when wild winds blow,
Our home is here, our hearts are one,
    Till Charles forgets to flow.
        Then old and young, etc.

BOSTON COMMON.—THREE PICTURES.

(FOR THE FAIR IN AID OF THE FUND TO PROCURE BALL'S STATUE OF WASHINGTON.)

1630.

ALL overgrown with bush and fern,
    And straggling clumps of tangled trees,
With trunks that lean and boughs that turn,
    Bent eastward by the mastering breeze, —
With spongy bogs that drip and fill
    A yellow pond with muddy rain,
Beneath the shaggy southern hill
    Lies wet and low the Shawmut plain.
And hark! the trodden branches crack;
    A crow flaps off with startled scream;
A straying woodchuck canters back;
    A bittern rises from the stream;
Leaps from his lair a frightened deer;
    An otter plunges in the pool; —
Here comes old Shawmut's pioneer,
    The parson on his brindled bull!

1774.

The streets are thronged with trampling feet,
    The northern hill is ridged with graves,
But night and morn the drum is beat
    To frighten down the " rebel knaves."
The stones of King Street still are red,
    And yet the bloody red-coats come :
I hear their pacing sentry's tread,
    The click of steel, the tap of drum,
And over all the open green,
    Where grazed of late the harmless kine,
The cannon's deepening ruts are seen,
    The war-horse stamps, the bayonets shine.
The clouds are dark with crimson rain
    Above the murderous hirelings' den,
And soon their whistling showers shall stain
    The pipe-clayed belts of Gage's men.

186 . . . . .

Around the green, in morning light,
    The spired and palaced summits blaze,
And, sunlike, from her Beacon-height
    The dome-crowned city spreads her rays ;

They span the waves, they belt the plains,
   They skirt the roads with bands of white,
Till with a flash of gilded panes
   Yon farthest hill-side bounds the sight.
Peace, Freedom, Wealth! no fairer view,
   Though with the wild-bird's restless wings
We sailed beneath the noontide's blue
   Or chased the moonlight's endless rings!
Here, fitly raised by grateful hands
   His holiest memory to recall,
The Hero's, Patriot's image stands;
   He led our sires who won them all!

November 14, 1859.

LATTER-DAY WARNINGS.

When legislators keep the law,
    When banks dispense with bolts and locks,
When berries — whortle, rasp, and straw —
    Grow bigger *downwards* through the box, —

When he that selleth house or land
    Shows leak in roof or flaw in right, —
When haberdashers choose the stand
    Whose window hath the broadest light, —

When preachers tell us all they think,
    And party leaders all they mean, —
When what we pay for, that we drink,
    From real grape and coffee-bean, —

When lawyers take what they would give,
   And doctors give what they would take, —
When city fathers eat to live,
   Save when they fast for conscience' sake, —

When one that hath a horse on sale
   Shall bring his merit to the proof,
Without a lie for every nail
   That holds the iron on the hoof, —

When in the usual place for rips
   Our gloves are stitched with special care,
And guarded well the whalebone tips
   Where first umbrellas need repair, —

When Cuba's weeds have quite forgot
   The power of suction to resist,
And claret-bottles harbor not
   Such dimples as would hold your fist, —

When publishers no longer steal,
   And pay for what they stole before, —
When the first locomotive's wheel
   Rolls through the Hoosac tunnel's bore; —

Till then let Cumming blaze away,
    And Miller's saints blow up the globe;
But when you see that blessed day,
    Then order your ascension robe!

PROLOGUE.

A Prologue? Well, of course the ladies know; —
I have my doubts. No matter, — here we go!
What is a Prologue? Let our Tutor teach:
Pro means beforehand; *logos* stands for speech.
'T is like the harper's prelude on the strings,
The prima donna's courtesy ere she sings: —
Prologues in metre are to other *pros*
As worsted stockings are to engine-hose.

"The world 's a stage," — as Shakespeare said, one day;
The stage a world — was what he meant to say.
The outside world 's a blunder, that is clear;
The real world that Nature meant is here.
Here every foundling finds its lost mamma;
Each rogue, repentant, melts his stern papa;
Misers relent, the spendthrift's debts are paid,

The cheats are taken in the traps they laid;
One after one the troubles all are past
Till the fifth act comes right side up at last,
When the young couple, old folks, rogues, and all,
Join hands, *so* happy at the curtain's fall.
Here suffering virtue ever finds relief,
And black-browed ruffians always come to grief.
When the lorn damsel, with a frantic screech,
And cheeks as hueless as a brandy-peach,
Cries, "Help, kyind Heaven!" and drops upon her knees
On the green — baize, — beneath the (canvas) trees, —
See to her side avenging Valor fly : —
"Ha! Villain! Draw! Now, Terraitorr, yield or die!"
When the poor hero flounders in despair,
Some dear lost uncle turns up millionnaire,
Clasps the young scapegrace with paternal joy,
Sobs on his neck, "*My boy!* My boy!! MY BOY!!!"

Ours, then, sweet friends, the real world to-night.
Of love that conquers in disaster's spite.
Ladies attend! While woful cares and doubt
Wrong the soft passion in the world without,
Though fortune scowl, though prudence interfere,
One thing is certain: Love will triumph here!

PROLOGUE.

Lords of creation, whom your ladies rule, —
The world's great masters, when you're out of school, —
Learn the brief moral of our evening's play:
Man has his will, — but woman has her way!
While man's dull spirit toils in smoke and fire,
Woman's swift instinct threads the electric wire, —
The magic bracelet stretched beneath the waves
Beats the black giant with his score of slaves.
All earthly powers confess your sovereign art
But that one rebel, — woman's wilful heart.
All foes you master; but a woman's wit
Lets daylight through you ere you know you're hit.
So, just to picture what her art can do,
Hear an old story, made as good as new.

Rudolph, professor of the headsman's trade,
Alike was famous for his arm and blade.
One day a prisoner Justice had to kill
Knelt at the block to test the artist's skill.
Bare-armed, swart-visaged, gaunt, and shaggy-browed,
Rudolph the headsman rose above the crowd.
His falchion lightened with a sudden gleam,
As the pike's armor flashes in the stream.
He sheathed his blade; he turned as if to go;
The victim knelt, still waiting for the blow.

"Why strikest not? Perform thy murderous act,"
The prisoner said. (His voice was slightly cracked.)
"Friend, I *have* struck," the artist straight replied;
"Wait but one moment, and yourself decide."
He held his snuff-box, — "Now then, if you please!"
The prisoner sniffed, and, with a crashing sneeze,
Off his head tumbled, — bowled along the floor, —
Bounced down the steps; — the prisoner said no more!

Woman! thy falchion is a glittering eye;
If death lurk in it, O, how sweet to die!
Thou takest hearts as Rudolph took the head;
We die with love, and never dream we're dead!

THE OLD MAN OF THE SEA.

A NIGHTMARE DREAM BY DAYLIGHT.

Do you know the Old Man of the Sea, of the Sea?
   Have you met with that dreadful old man?
If you have n't been caught, you will be, you will be;
   For catch you he must and he can.

He does n't hold on by your throat, by your throat,
   As of old in the terrible tale;
But he grapples you tight by the coat, by the coat,
   Till its buttons and button-holes fail.

There's the charm of a snake in his eye, in his eye,
   And a polypus-grip in his hands;
You cannot go back, nor get by, nor get by,
   If you look at the spot where he stands.

O, you 're grabbed! See his claw on your sleeve, on your sleeve!
   It is Sinbad's Old Man of the Sea!

You're a Christian, no doubt you believe, you believe:
  You're a martyr, whatever you be!

— Is the breakfast-hour past? They must wait, they must wait,
  While the coffee boils sullenly down,
While the Johnny-cake burns on the grate, on the grate,
  And the toast is done frightfully brown.

— Yes, your dinner will keep; let it cool, let it cool,
  And Madam may worry and fret,
And children half-starved go to school, go to school;
  He can't think of sparing you yet.

— Hark! the bell for the train! "Come along! Come along!
  For there is n't a second to lose."
"ALL ABOARD!" (He holds on.) "Fsht! ding-dong! Fsht! ding-dong!" —
  You can follow on foot, if you choose.

— There's a maid with a cheek like a peach, like a peach,
  That is waiting for you in the church; —
But he clings to your side like a leech, like a leech,
  And you leave your lost bride in the lurch.

— There's a babe in a fit, — hurry quick! hurry quick!
   To the doctor's as fast as you can!
The baby is off, while you stick, while you stick,
   In the grip of the dreadful Old Man!

— I have looked on the face of the Bore, of the Bore;
   The voice of the Simple I know;
I have welcomed the Flat at my door, at my door;
   I have sat by the side of the Slow;

I have walked like a lamb by the friend, by the friend,
   That stuck to my skirts like a burr;
I have borne the stale talk without end, without end,
   Of the sitter whom nothing could stir:

But my hamstrings grow loose, and I shake, and I shake,
   At the sight of the dreadful Old Man;
Yea, I quiver and quake, and I take, and I take,
   To my legs with what vigor I can!

O the dreadful Old Man of the Sea, of the Sea!
   He's come back like the Wandering Jew!
He has had his cold claw upon me, upon me, —
   And be sure that he'll have it on you!

ODE FOR A SOCIAL MEETING.

WITH SLIGHT ALTERATIONS BY A TEETOTALER.

Come! fill a fresh bumper, — for why should we go
While the ~~nectar~~ ^{logwood} still reddens our cups as they flow?
Pour out the ~~rich juices~~ ^{decoction} still bright with the sun,
Till o'er the brimmed crystal the ~~rubies~~ ^{dye-stuff} shall run.

The ~~purple-globed clusters~~ ^{half-ripened apples} their life-dews have bled;
How sweet is the ~~breath~~ ^{taste} of the ~~fragrance they shed~~ ^{sugar of lead}!
For summer's ~~last roses~~ ^{rank poisons} lie hid in the ~~wines~~ ^{wines!!!}
That were garnered by ~~maidens who laughed thro' the vines.~~ ^{stable-boys smoking long-nines}

Then a ~~smile~~ ^{scowl}, and a ~~glass~~ ^{howl}, and a ~~toast~~ ^{scoff}, and a ~~cheer~~ ^{sneer},
For ~~all the good wine, and we've some of it here~~ ^{strychnine and whiskey, and ratsbane and beer}!
In cellar, in pantry, in attic, in hall,
~~Long live the gay servant that laughs for us all!~~ ^{Down, down with the tyrant that masters us all!}

THE DEACON'S MASTERPIECE:

OR THE WONDERFUL "ONE-HOSS SHAY."

A LOGICAL STORY.

HAVE you heard of the wonderful one-hoss shay,
That was built in such a logical way
It ran a hundred years to a day,
And then, of a sudden, it —— ah, but stay,
I'll tell you what happened without delay,
Scaring the parson into fits,
Frightening people out of their wits, —
Have you ever heard of that, I say?

Seventeen hundred and fifty-five.
Georgius Secundus was then alive, —
Snuffy old drone from the German hive.
That was the year when Lisbon-town
Saw the earth open and gulp her down,
And Braddock's army was done so brown,
Left without a scalp to its crown.

It was on the terrible Earthquake-day
That the Deacon finished the one-hoss shay.

Now in building of chaises, I tell you what,
There is always *somewhere* a weakest spot, —
In hub, tire, felloe, in spring or thill,
In panel, or crossbar, or floor, or sill,
In screw, bolt, thoroughbrace, — lurking still,
Find it somewhere you must and will, —
Above or below, or within or without, —
And that's the reason, beyond a doubt,
A chaise *breaks down*, but does n't *wear out*.

But the Deacon swore, (as Deacons do,
With an "I dew vum," or an "I tell *yeou*,")
He would build one shay to beat the taown
'n' the keounty 'n' all the kentry raoun';
It should be so built that it *couldn'* break daown:
— "Fur," said the Deacon, "'t's mighty plain
Thut the weakes' place mus' stan' the strain;
'n' the way t' fix it, uz I maintain,
      Is only jest
T' make that place uz strong uz the rest."

So the Deacon inquired of the village folk
Where he could find the strongest oak,

That could n't be split nor bent nor broke,—
That was for spokes and floor and sills;
He sent for lancewood to make the thills;
The crossbars were ash, from the straightest trees;
The panels of white-wood, that cuts like cheese,
But lasts like iron for things like these;
The hubs of logs from the "Settler's ellum,"—
Last of its timber,—they could n't sell 'em,
Never an axe had seen their chips,
And the wedges flew from between their lips,
Their blunt ends frizzled like celery-tips;
Step and prop-iron, bolt and screw,
Spring, tire, axle, and linchpin too,
Steel of the finest, bright and blue;
Thoroughbrace bison-skin, thick and wide;
Boot, top, dasher, from tough old hide
Found in the pit when the tanner died.
That was the way he "put her through."—
"There!" said the Deacon, "naow she 'll dew!"

Do! I tell you, I rather guess
She was a wonder, and nothing less!
Colts grew horses, beards turned gray,
Deacon and deaconess dropped away,
Children and grandchildren — where were they?

But there stood the stout old one-hoss shay
As fresh as on Lisbon-earthquake-day!

EIGHTEEN HUNDRED;— it came and found
The Deacon's masterpiece strong and sound.
Eighteen hundred increased by ten;—
"Hahnsum kerridge" they called it then.
Eighteen hundred and twenty came;—
Running as usual; much the same.
Thirty and forty at last arrive,
And then come fifty, and FIFTY-FIVE.

Little of all we value here
Wakes on the morn of its hundredth year
Without both feeling and looking queer.
In fact, there's nothing that keeps its youth,
So far as I know, but a tree and truth.
(This is a moral that runs at large;
Take it. — You're welcome. — No extra charge.)

FIRST OF NOVEMBER, — the Earthquake-day. —
There are traces of age in the one-hoss shay,
A general flavor of mild decay,
But nothing local as one may say.
There could n't be, — for the Deacon's art

Had made it so like in every part
That there was n't a chance for one to start.
For the wheels were just as strong as the thills,
And the floor was just as strong as the sills,
And the panels just as strong as the floor,
And the whippletree neither less nor more,
And the back-crossbar as strong as the fore,
And spring and axle and hub *encore.*
And yet, *as a whole,* it is past a doubt
In another hour it will be **worn out!**

First of November, 'Fifty-five!
This morning the parson takes a drive.
Now, small boys, get out of the way!
Here comes the wonderful one-hoss shay,
Drawn by a rat-tailed, ewe-necked bay.
"Huddup!" said the parson. — Off went they.

The parson was working his Sunday's text, —
Had got to *fifthly,* and stopped perplexed
At what the — Moses — was coming next.
All at once the horse stood still,
Close by the meet'n'-house on the hill.
— First a shiver, and then a thrill,
Then something decidedly like a spill, —

And the parson was sitting upon a rock,
At half past nine by the meet'n'-house clock, —
Just the hour of the Earthquake shock!
— What do you think the parson found,
When he got up and stared around?
The poor old chaise in a heap or mound,
As if it had been to the mill and ground!
You see, of course, if you 're not a dunce,
How it went to pieces all at once, —
All at once, and nothing first, —
Just as bubbles do when they burst.

End of the wonderful one-hoss shay.
Logic is logic. That 's all I say.

ÆSTIVATION.

AN UNPUBLISHED POEM, BY MY LATE LATIN TUTOR.

In candent ire the solar splendor flames;
The foles, languescent, pend from arid rames;
His humid front the cive, anheling, wipes,
And dreams of erring on ventiferous ripes.

How dulce to vive occult to mortal eyes,
Dorm on the herb with none to supervise,
Carp the suave berries from the crescent vine,
And bibe the flow from longicaudate kine!

To me, alas! no verdurous visions come,
Save yon exiguous pool's conferva-scum, —
No concave vast repeats the tender hue
That laves my milk-jug with celestial blue!

Me wretched! Let me curr to quercine shades!
Effund your albid hausts, lactiferous maids!
O, might I vole to some umbrageous clump, —
Depart, — be off, — excede, — evade, — erump!

CONTENTMENT.

" Man wants but little here below."

LITTLE I ask; my wants are few;
   I only wish a hut of stone,
(A *very plain* brown stone will do,)
      That I may call my own; —
And close at hand is such a one,
In yonder street that fronts the sun.

Plain food is quite enough for me;
   Three courses are as good as ten; —
If Nature can subsist on three,
      Thank Heaven for three. Amen!
I always thought cold victual nice; —
My *choice* would be vanilla-ice.

I care not much for gold or land; —
   Give me a mortgage here and there, —

Some good bank stock, — some note of hand,
        Or trifling railroad share ; —
I only ask that Fortune send
A *little* more than I shall spend.

Honors are silly toys, I know,
    And titles are but empty names ;
I would, *perhaps*, be Plenipo, —
        But only near St. James ;
I 'm very sure I should not care
To fill our Gubernator's chair.

Jewels are bawbles ; 't is a sin
    To care for such unfruitful things ; —
One good-sized diamond in a pin, —
        Some, *not so large*, in rings, —
A ruby, and a pearl, or so,
Will do for me ; — I laugh at show.

My dame should dress in cheap attire ;
    (Good, heavy silks are never dear ;) —
I own perhaps I *might* desire
        Some shawls of true Cashmere, —
Some marrowy crapes of China silk,
Like wrinkled skins on scalded milk.

I would not have the horse I drive
   So fast that folks must stop and stare;
An easy gait — two, forty-five —
      Suits me; I do not care; —
Perhaps, for just a *single spurt*,
Some seconds less would do no hurt.

Of pictures, I should like to own
   Titians and Raphaels three or four, —
I love so much their style and tone, —
      One Turner, and no more,
(A landscape, — foreground golden dirt, —
The sunshine painted with a squirt.)

Of books but few, — some fifty score
   For daily use, and bound for wear;
The rest upon an upper floor; —
      Some *little* luxury *there*
Of red morocco's gilded gleam,
And vellum rich as country cream.

Busts, cameos, gems, — such things as these,
   Which others often show for pride,
I value for their power to please,
      And selfish churls deride; —

One Stradivarius, I confess,
Two Meerschaums, I would fain possess.

Wealth's wasteful tricks I will not learn,
   Nor ape the glittering upstart fool; —
Shall not carved tables serve my turn,
   But *all* must be of buhl?
Give grasping pomp its double share, —
I ask but *one* recumbent chair.

Thus humble let me live and die,
   Nor long for Midas' golden touch;
If Heaven more generous gifts deny,
     I shall not miss them *much*, —
Too grateful for the blessing lent
Of simple tastes and mind content!

PARSON TURELL'S LEGACY:

OR, THE PRESIDENT'S OLD ARM-CHAIR.

A MATHEMATICAL STORY.

FACTS respecting an old arm-chair.
At Cambridge. Is kept in the College there.
Seems but little the worse for wear.
That's remarkable when I say
It was old in President Holyoke's day.
(One of his boys, perhaps you know,
Died, *at one hundred*, years ago.)
He took lodgings for rain or shine
Under green bed-clothes in '69.

Know old Cambridge? Hope you do. —
Born there? Don't say so! I was, too.
(Born in a house with a gambrel-roof, —
Standing still, if you must have proof. —

"Gambrel? — Gambrel?" — Let me beg
You'll look at a horse's hinder leg, —
First great angle above the hoof, —
That's the gambrel; hence gambrel-roof.)
— Nicest place that ever was seen, —
Colleges red and Common green,
Sidewalks brownish with trees between.
Sweetest spot beneath the skies
When the canker-worms don't rise, —
When the dust, that sometimes flies
Into your mouth and ears and eyes,
In a quiet slumber lies,
Not in the shape of unbaked pies
Such as barefoot children prize.

A kind of harbor it seems to be,
Facing the flow of a boundless sea.
Rows of gray old Tutors stand
Ranged like rocks above the sand;
Rolling beneath them, soft and green,
Breaks the tide of bright sixteen, —
One wave, two waves, three waves, four,
Sliding up the sparkling floor:
Then it ebbs to flow no more,
Wandering off from shore to shore

With its freight of golden ore!
— Pleasant place for boys to play; —
Better keep your girls away;
Hearts get rolled as pebbles do
Which countless fingering waves pursue,
And every classic beach is strown
With heart-shaped pebbles of blood-red stone.

But this is neither here nor there; —
I'm talking about an old arm-chair.
You've heard, no doubt, of PARSON TURELL?
Over at Medford he used to dwell;
Married one of the Mathers' folk;
Got with his wife a chair of oak, —
Funny old chair with seat like wedge,
Sharp behind and broad front edge, —
One of the oddest of human things,
Turned all over with knobs and rings, —
But heavy, and wide, and deep, and grand, —
Fit for the worthies of the land, —
Chief-Justice Sewall a cause to try in,
Or Cotton Mather to sit — and lie — in.
— Parson Turell bequeathed the same
To a certain student, — SMITH by name;
These were the terms, as we are told:

"Saide Smith saide Chaire to have and holde;
When he doth graduate, then to passe
To ye oldest Youth in ye Senior Classe.
On Payment of" — (naming a certain sum) —
" By him to whom ye Chaire shall come ;
He to ye oldest Senior next,
And soe forever," — (thus runs the text,) —
" But one Crown lesse then he gave to claime,
That being his Debte for use of same."

Smith transferred it to one of the BROWNS,
And took his money, — five silver crowns.
Brown delivered it up to MOORE,
Who paid, it is plain, not five, but four.
Moore made over the chair to LEE,
Who gave him crowns of silver three.
Lee conveyed it unto DREW,
And now the payment, of course, was two.
Drew gave up the chair to DUNN, —
All he got, as you see, was one.
Dunn released the chair to HALL,
And got by the bargain no crown at all.
— And now it passed to a second BROWN,
Who took it and likewise *claimed a crown.*
When *Brown* conveyed it unto WARE,

Having had one crown, to make it fair,
He paid him two crowns to take the chair;
And *Ware*, being honest, (as all Wares be,)
He paid one POTTER, who took it, three.
Four got ROBINSON; five got DIX;
JOHNSON *primus* demanded six;
And so the sum kept gathering still
Till after the battle of Bunker's Hill.

— When paper money became so cheap,
Folks would n't count it, but said " a heap,"
A certain RICHARDS, — the books declare, —
(A. M. in '90 ? I've looked with care
Through the Triennial, — *name not there.*)
This person, Richards, was offered then
Eight score pounds, but would have ten;
Nine, I think, was the sum he took, —
Not quite certain, — but see the book.

— By and by the wars were still,
But nothing had altered the Parson's will.
The old arm-chair was solid yet,
But saddled with such a monstrous debt!
Things grew quite too bad to bear,
Paying such sums to get rid of the chair!
But dead men's fingers hold awful tight,
And there was the will in black and white,

Plain enough for a child to spell.
What should be done no man could tell,
For the chair was a kind of nightmare curse,
And every season but made it worse.

  As a last resort, to clear the doubt,
They got old GOVERNOR HANCOCK out.
The Governor came with his Light-horse Troop
And his mounted truckmen, all cock-a-hoop;
Halberds glittered and colors flew,
French horns whinnied and trumpets blew,
The yellow fifes whistled between their teeth
And the bumble-bee bass-drums boomed beneath;
So he rode with all his band,
Till the President met him, cap in hand.
— The Governor "hefted" the crowns, and said, —
"A will is a will, and the Parson's dead."
The Governor hefted the crowns. Said he, —
"There is your p'int. And here's my fee.
These are the terms you must fulfil, —
On such conditions I BREAK THE WILL!"
The Governor mentioned what these should be.
(Just wait a minute and then you 'll see.)
The President prayed. Then all was still,
And the Governor rose and BROKE THE WILL!

—"About those conditions?" Well, now you go
And do as I tell you, and then you'll know.
Once a year, on Commencement day,
If you'll only take the pains to stay,
You'll see the President in the CHAIR,
Likewise the Governor sitting there.
The President rises; both old and young
May hear his speech in a foreign tongue,
The meaning whereof, as lawyers swear,
Is this: Can I keep this old arm-chair?
And then his Excellency bows,
As much as to say that he allows.
The Vice-Gub. next is called by name;
He bows like t' other, which means the same.
And all the officers round 'em bow,
As much as to say that *they* allow.
And a lot of parchments about the chair
Are handed to witnesses then and there,
And then the lawyers hold it clear
That the chair is safe for another year.

God bless you, Gentlemen! Learn to give
Money to colleges while you live.
Don't be silly and think you'll try
To bother the colleges, when you die,

With codicil this, and codicil that,
That Knowledge may starve while Law grows fat;
For there never was pitcher that would n't spill,
And there's always a flaw in a donkey's will!

DE SAUTY.

AN ELECTRO-CHEMICAL ECLOGUE.

Professor.   *Blue-Nose.*

PROFESSOR.

TELL me, O Provincial! speak, Ceruleo-Nasal!
Lives there one De Sauty extant now among you,
Whispering Boanerges, son of silent thunder,
    Holding talk with nations?

Is there a De Sauty ambulant on Tellus,
Bifid-cleft like mortals, dormient in night-cap,
Having sight, smell, hearing, food-receiving feature
    Three times daily patent?

Breathes there such a being, O Ceruleo-Nasal?
Or is he a *mythus*, — ancient word for "humbug,"—
Such as Livy told about the wolf that wet-nursed
    Romulus and Remus?

Was he born of woman, this alleged De Sauty?
Or a living product of galvanic action,
Like the *acarus* bred in Crosse's flint-solution?
    Speak, thou Cyano-Rhinal!

BLUE-NOSE.

Many things thou askest, jackknife-bearing stranger,
Much-conjecturing mortal, pork-and-treacle-waster!
Pretermit thy whittling, wheel thine ear-flap toward me,
    Thou shalt hear them answered.

When the charge galvanic tingled through the cable,
At the polar focus of the wire electric
Suddenly appeared a white-faced man among us:
    Called himself " DE SAUTY."

As the small opossum held in pouch maternal
Grasps the nutrient organ whence the term *mammalia*,
So the unknown stranger held the wire electric,
    Sucking in the current.

When the current strengthened, bloomed the pale-faced
    stranger, —
Took no drink nor victual, yet grew fat and rosy, —
And from time to time, in sharp articulation,
    Said, " *All right!* DE SAUTY."

From the lonely station passed the utterance, spreading
Through the pines and hemlocks to the groves of steeples,
Till the land was filled with loud reverberations
    Of "*All right!* DE SAUTY."

When the current slackened, drooped the mystic stran-
      ger, —
Faded, faded, faded, as the stream grew weaker, —
Wasted to a shadow, with a hartshorn odor
    Of disintegration.

Drops of deliquescence glistened on his forehead,
Whitened round his feet the dust of efflorescence,
Till one Monday morning, when the flow suspended,
    There was no De Sauty.

Nothing but a cloud of elements organic,
C. O. H. N. Ferrum, Chlor. Flu. Sil. Potassa,
Calc. Sod. Phosph. Mag. Sulphur, Mang. (?) Alumin. (?)
    Cuprum, (?)
    Such as man is made of.

Born of stream galvanic, with it he had perished!
There is no De Sauty now there is no current!
Give us a new cable, then again we'll hear him
    Cry, "*All right!* DE SAUTY."

THE OLD MAN DREAMS.

O FOR one hour of youthful joy!
    Give back my twentieth spring!
I'd rather laugh a bright-haired boy
    Than reign a gray-beard king!

Off with the wrinkled spoils of age!
    Away with learning's crown!
Tear out life's wisdom-written page,
    And dash its trophies down!

One moment let my life-blood stream
    From boyhood's fount of flame!
Give me one giddy, reeling dream
    Of life all love and fame!

— My listening angel heard the prayer,
    And, calmly smiling, said,
"If I but touch thy silvered hair,
    Thy hasty wish hath sped.

"But is there nothing in thy track
    To bid thee fondly stay,
While the swift seasons hurry back
    To find the wished-for day?"

— Ah, truest soul of womankind!
    Without thee, what were life?
One bliss I cannot leave behind:
    I'll take — my — precious — wife!

— The angel took a sapphire pen
    And wrote in rainbow dew,
"The man would be a boy again,
    And be a husband too!"

— "And is there nothing yet unsaid
    Before the change appears?
Remember, all their gifts have fled
    With those dissolving years!"

Why, yes; for memory would recall
   My fond paternal joys;
I could not bear to leave them all;
   I 'll take — my — girl — and — boys!

The smiling angel dropped his pen, —
   " Why this will never do;
The man would be a boy again,
   And be a father too!"

And so I laughed, — my laughter woke
   The household with its noise, —
And wrote my dream, when morning broke,
   To please the gray-haired boys.

MARE RUBRUM.

Flash out a stream of blood-red wine! —
    For I would drink to other days;
And brighter shall their memory shine,
    Seen flaming through its crimson blaze.
The roses die, the summers fade;
    But every ghost of boyhood's dream
By Nature's magic power is laid
    To sleep beneath this blood-red stream.

It filled the purple grapes that lay
    And drank the splendors of the sun
Where the long summer's cloudless day
    Is mirrored in the broad Garonne;
It pictures still the bacchant shapes
    That saw their hoarded sunlight shed, —
The maidens dancing on the grapes, —
    Their milk-white ankles splashed with red.

Beneath these waves of crimson lie,
   In rosy fetters prisoned fast,
Those flitting shapes that never die,
   The swift-winged visions of the past.
Kiss but the crystal's mystic rim,
   Each shadow rends its flowery chain,
Springs in a bubble from its brim
   And walks the chambers of the brain.

Poor Beauty! time and fortune's wrong
   No form nor feature may withstand, —
Thy wrecks are scattered all along,
   Like emptied sea-shells on the sand; —
Yet, sprinkled with this blushing rain,
   The dust restores each blooming girl,
As if the sea-shells moved again
   Their glistening lips of pink and pearl.

Here lies the home of schoolboy life,
   With creaking stair and wind-swept hall,
And, scarred by many a truant knife,
   Our old initials on the wall;
Here rest — their keen vibrations mute —
   The shout of voices known so well,
The ringing laugh, the wailing flute,
   The chiding of the sharp-tongued bell.

Here, clad in burning robes, are laid
　　Life's blossomed joys, untimely shed;
And here those cherished forms have strayed
　　We miss awhile, and call them dead.
What wizard fills the maddening glass?
　　What soil the enchanted clusters grew,
That buried passions wake and pass
　　In beaded drops of fiery dew?

Nay, take the cup of blood-red wine,—
　　Our hearts can boast a warmer glow,
Filled from a vintage more divine,—
　　Calmed, but not chilled by winter's snow!
To-night the palest wave we sip
　　Rich as the priceless draught shall be
That wet the bride of Cana's lip,—
　　The wedding wine of Galilee!

WHAT WE ALL THINK.

That age was older once than now,
    In spite of locks untimely shed,
Or silvered on the youthful brow ;
    That babes make love and children wed.

That sunshine had a heavenly glow,
    Which faded with those " good old days "
When winters came with deeper snow,
    And autumns with a softer haze.

That — mother, sister, wife, or child —
    The " best of women " each has known.
Were schoolboys ever half so wild?
    How young the grandpapas have grown!

That *but for this* our souls were free,
    And *but for that* our lives were blest;
That in some season yet to be
    Our cares will leave us time to rest.

Whene'er we groan with ache or pain, —
    Some common ailment of the race, —
Though doctors think the matter plain, —
    That ours is " a peculiar case."

That when like babes with fingers burned
    We count one bitter maxim more,
Our lesson all the world has learned,
    And men are wiser than before.

That when we sob o'er fancied woes,
    The angels hovering overhead
Count every pitying drop that flows
    And love us for the tears we shed.

That when we stand with tearless eye
    And turn the beggar from our door,
They still approve us when we sigh,
    " Ah, had I but *one thousand more!* "

Though temples crowd the crumbled brink
  O'erhanging truth's eternal flow,
Their tablets bold with *what we think*,
  Their echoes dumb to *what we know;*

That one unquestioned text we read,
  All doubt beyond, all fear above,
Nor crackling pile nor cursing creed
  Can burn or blot it: GOD IS LOVE!

SPRING HAS COME.

INTRA MUROS.

The sunbeams, lost for half a year,
    Slant through my pane their morning rays;
For dry northwesters cold and clear,
    The east blows in its thin blue haze.

And first the snowdrop's bells are seen,
    Then close against the sheltering wall
The tulip's horn of dusky green,
    The peony's dark unfolding ball.

The golden-chaliced crocus burns;
    The long narcissus-blades appear;
The cone-beaked hyacinth returns
    To light her blue-flamed chandelier.

The willow's whistling lashes, wrung
    By the wild winds of gusty March,
With sallow leaflets lightly strung,
    Are swaying by the tufted larch.

The elms have robed their slender spray
    With full-blown flower and embryo leaf;
Wide o'er the clasping arch of day
    Soars like a cloud their hoary chief.

See the proud tulip's flaunting cup,
    That flames in glory for an hour, —
Behold it withering, — then look up, —
    How meek the forest monarch's flower!

When wake the violets, Winter dies;
    When sprout the elm-buds, Spring is near;
When lilacs blossom, Summer cries,
    "Bud, little roses! Spring is here!"

The windows blush with fresh bouquets,
    Cut with the May-dew on their lips;
The radish all its bloom displays,
    Pink as Aurora's finger-tips.

Nor less the flood of light that showers
    On beauty's changed corolla-shades, —
The walks are gay as bridal bowers
    With rows of many-petalled maids.

The scarlet shell-fish click and clash
    In the blue barrow where they slide;
The horseman, proud of streak and splash,
    Creeps homeward from his morning ride.

Here comes the dealer's awkward string,
    With neck in rope and tail in knot, —
Rough colts, with careless country-swing,
    In lazy walk or slouching trot.

—— Wild filly from the mountain-side,
    Doomed to the close and chafing thills,
Lend me thy long, untiring stride
    To seek with thee thy western hills!

I hear the whispering voice of Spring,
    The thrush's trill, the robin's cry,
Like some poor bird with prisoned wing
    That sits and sings, but longs to fly.

O for one spot of living green, —
   One little spot where leaves can grow, —
To love unblamed, to walk unseen,
   To dream above, to sleep below!

A GOOD TIME GOING!

Brave singer of the coming time,
   Sweet minstrel of the joyous present,
Crowned with the noblest wreath of rhyme,
   The holly-leaf of Ayrshire's peasant,
Good by! Good by! — Our hearts and hands,
   Our lips in honest Saxon phrases,
Cry, God be with him, till he stands
   His feet among the English daisies!

'T is here we part; — for other eyes
   The busy deck, the fluttering streamer,
The dripping arms that plunge and rise,
   The waves in foam, the ship in tremor,
The kerchiefs waving from the pier,
   The cloudy pillar gliding o'er him,
The deep blue desert, lone and drear,
   With heaven above and home before him!

His home! — the Western giant smiles,
    And twirls the spotty globe to find it; —
This little speck the British Isles?
    'T is but a freckle, — never mind it!
He laughs, and all his prairies roll,
    Each gurgling cataract roars and chuckles,
And ridges stretched from pole to pole
    Heave till they crack their iron knuckles!

But Memory blushes at the sneer,
    And Honor turns with frown defiant,
And Freedom, leaning on her spear,
    Laughs louder than the laughing giant:
" An islet is a world," she said,
    " When glory with its dust has blended,
And Britain keeps her noble dead
    Till earth and seas and skies are rended!"

Beneath each swinging forest-bough
    Some arm as stout in death reposes, —
From wave-washed foot to heaven-kissed brow
    Her valor's life-blood runs in roses;
Nay, let our brothers of the West
    Write smiling in their florid pages,
One half her soil has walked the rest
    In poets, heroes, martyrs, sages!

Hugged in the clinging billow's clasp,
    From sea-weed fringe to mountain heather,
The British oak with rooted grasp
    Her slender handful holds together; —
With cliffs of white and bowers of green,
    And Ocean narrowing to caress her,
And hills and threaded streams between, —
    Our little mother isle, God bless her!

In earth's broad temple where we stand,
    Fanned by the eastern gales that brought us,
We hold the missal in our hand,
    Bright with the lines our Mother taught us;
Where'er its blazoned page betrays
    The glistening links of gilded fetters,
Behold, the half-turned leaf displays
    Her rubric stained in crimson letters!

Enough! To speed a parting friend
    'T is vain alike to speak and listen; —
Yet stay, — these feeble accents blend
    With rays of light from eyes that glisten.
Good by! once more, — and kindly tell
    In words of peace the young world's story, —
And say, besides, we love too well
    Our mothers' soil, our fathers' glory!

THE LAST BLOSSOM.

Though young no more, we still would dream
    Of beauty's dear deluding wiles;
The leagues of life to graybeards seem
    Shorter than boyhood's lingering miles.

Who knows a woman's wild caprice?
    It played with Goethe's silvered hair,
And many a Holy Father's "niece"
    Has softly smoothed the papal chair.

When sixty bids us sigh in vain
    To melt the heart of sweet sixteen,
We think upon those ladies twain
    Who loved so well the tough old Dean.

We see the Patriarch's wintry face,
    The maid of Egypt's dusky glow,
And dream that Youth and Age embrace,
    As April violets fill with snow.

Tranced in her lord's Olympian smile
    His lotus-loving Memphian lies, —
The musky daughter of the Nile,
    With plaited hair and almond eyes.

Might we but share one wild caress
    Ere life's autumnal blossoms fall,
And Earth's brown, clinging lips impress
    The long cold kiss that waits us all!

My bosom heaves, remembering yet
    The morning of that blissful day,
When Rose, the flower of spring, I met,
    And gave my raptured soul away.

Flung from her eyes of purest blue,
    A lasso, with its leaping chain,
Light as a loop of larkspurs, flew
    O'er sense and spirit, heart and brain.

Thou com'st to cheer my waning age,
    Sweet vision, waited for so long!
Dove that would seek the poet's cage
    Lured by the magic breath of song!

She blushes! Ah, reluctant maid,
    Love's *drapeau rouge* the truth has told!
O'er girlhood's yielding barricade
    Floats the great Leveller's crimson fold!

Come to my arms! — love heeds not years;
    No frost the bud of passion knows. —
Ha! what is this my frenzy hears?
    A voice behind me uttered, — Rose!

Sweet was her smile, — but not for me;
    Alas! when woman looks *too* kind,
Just turn your foolish head and see, —
    Some youth is walking close behind!

"THE BOYS."

Has there any old fellow got mixed with the boys?
If there has, take him out, without making a noise.
Hang the Almanac's cheat and the Catalogue's spite!
Old time is a liar! We're twenty to-night!

We're twenty! We're twenty! Who says we are more?
He's tipsy, — young jackanapes! — show him the door!
"Gray temples at twenty?" — Yes! *white* if we please;
Where the snow-flakes fall thickest there's nothing can freeze!

Was it snowing I spoke of? Excuse the mistake!
Look close, — you will see not a sign of a flake!

We want some new garlands for those we have shed, —
And these are white roses in place of the red.

We 've a trick, we young fellows, you may have been told,
Of talking (in public) as if we were old : —
That boy we call " Doctor," and this we call " Judge";
It 's a neat little fiction, — of course it 's all fudge.

That fellow 's the " Speaker," — the one on the right;
" Mr. Mayor," my young one, how are you to-night?
That 's our " Member of Congress," we say when we chaff;
There 's the " Reverend " What 's his name ? — do n't make me laugh.

That boy with the grave mathematical look
Made believe he had written a wonderful book,
And the ROYAL SOCIETY thought it was *true!*
So they chose him right in, — a good joke it was too!

There 's a boy, we pretend, with a three-decker brain,
That could harness a team with a logical chain;
When he spoke for our manhood in syllabled fire,
We called him " The Justice," but now he 's " The Squire."

And there's a nice youngster of excellent pith, —
Fate tried to conceal him by naming him Smith;
But he shouted a song for the brave and the free, —
Just read on his medal, "My country," "of thee!"

You hear that boy laughing? — You think he's all fun;
But the angels laugh, too, at the good he has done;
The children laugh loud as they troop to his call,
And the poor man that knows him laughs loudest of all!

Yes, we're boys, — always playing with tongue or with
    pen;
And I sometimes have asked, Shall we ever be men?
Shall we always be youthful, and laughing, and gay,
Till the last dear companion drops smiling away?

Then here's to our boyhood, its gold and its gray!
The stars of its winter, the dews of its May!
And when we have done with our life-lasting toys,
Dear Father, take care of thy children, THE BOYS!

    January 6, 1859.

THE OPENING OF THE PIANO.

In the little southern parlor of the house you may have
    seen
With the gambrel-roof, and the gable looking westward
    to the green,
At the side toward the sunset, with the window on its
    right,
Stood the London-made piano I am dreaming of to-night!

Ah me! how I remember the evening when it came!
What a cry of eager voices, what a group of cheeks in
    flame,
When the wondrous box was opened that had come
    from over seas,
With its smell of mastic-varnish and its flash of ivory
    keys!

Then the children all grew fretful in the restlessness of joy,
For the boy would push his sister, and the sister crowd the boy,
Till the father asked for quiet in his grave paternal way,
But the mother hushed the tumult with the words, "Now, Mary, play."

For the dear soul knew that music was a very sovereign balm ;
She had sprinkled it over Sorrow and seen its brow grow calm,
In the days of slender harpsichords with tapping tinkling quills,
Or carolling to her spinet with its thin metallic thrills.

So Mary, the household minstrel, who always loved to please,
Sat down to the new "Clementi," and struck the glittering keys.
Hushed were the children's voices, and every eye grew dim,
As, floating from lip and finger, arose the "Vesper Hymn."

— Catharine, child of a neighbor, curly and rosy-red,
(Wedded since, and a widow, — something like ten
    years dead,)
Hearing a gush of music such as none before,
Steals from her mother's chamber and peeps at the
    open door.

Just as the " Jubilate " in threaded whisper dies,
"Open it! open it, lady!" the little maiden cries,
(For she thought 't was a singing creature caged in a
    box she heard,)
" Open it! open it, lady! and let me see the *bird!* "

MIDSUMMER.

Here! sweep these foolish leaves away, —
I will not crush my brains to-day!
Look! are the southern curtains drawn?
Fetch me a fan, and so begone!

Not that, — the palm-trees rustling leaf
Brought from a parching coral-reef!
Its breath is heated; — I would swing
The broad gray plumes, — the eagle's wing.

I hate these roses' feverish blood! —
Pluck me a half-blown lily-bud,
A long-stemmed lily from the lake,
Cold as a coiling water-snake.

Rain me sweet odors on the air,
And wheel me up my Indian chair,
And spread some book not overwise
Flat out before my sleepy eyes.

— Who knows it not, — this dead recoil
Of weary fibres stretched with toil, —
The pulse that flutters faint and low
When Summer's seething breezes blow?

O Nature! bare thy loving breast,
And give thy child one hour of rest, —
One little hour to lie unseen
Beneath thy scarf of leafy green!

So, curtained by a singing pine,
Its murmuring voice shall blend with mine,
Till, lost in dreams, my faltering lay
In sweeter music dies away.

A PARTING HEALTH.

TO J. L. MOTLEY.

Yes, we knew we must lose him, — though friendship may claim
To blend her green leaves with the laurels of fame;
Though fondly, at parting, we call him our own,
'T is the whisper of love when the bugle has blown.

As the rider that rests with the spur on his heel, —
As the guardsman that sleeps in his corselet of steel, —
As the archer that stands with his shaft on the string,
He stoops from his toil to the garland we bring.

What pictures yet slumber unborn in his loom,
Till their warriors shall breathe and their beauties shall bloom,
While the tapestry lengthens the life-glowing dyes
That caught from our sunsets the stain of their skies!

In the alcoves of death, in the charnels of time,
Where flit the gaunt spectres of passion and crime,
There are triumphs untold, there are martyrs unsung,
There are heroes yet silent to speak with his tongue!

Let us hear the proud story which time has bequeathed!
From lips that are warm with the freedom they breathed!
Let him summon its tyrants, and tell us their doom,
Though he sweep the black past like Van Tromp with his broom!

*   *   *   *   *

The dream flashes by, for the west-winds awake
On pampas, on prairie, o'er mountain and lake,
To bathe the swift bark, like a sea-girdled shrine,
With incense they stole from the rose and the pine.

So fill a bright cup with the sunlight that gushed
When the dead summer's jewels were trampled and crushed:
THE TRUE KNIGHT OF LEARNING, — the world holds him dear, —
Love bless him, Joy crown him, God speed his career!

1857.

A GOOD-BY.

TO J. R. LOWELL.

FAREWELL, for the bark has her breast to the tide,
And the rough arms of Ocean are stretched for his bride;
The winds from the mountain stream over the bay;
One clasp of the hand, then away and away!

I see the tall mast as it rocks by the shore;
The sun is declining, I see it once more;
To-day like the blade in a thick-waving field,
To-morrow the spike on a Highlander's shield.

Alone, while the cloud pours its treacherous breath,
With the blue lips all round her whose kisses are death;
Ah, think not the breeze that is urging her sail
Has left her unaided to strive with the gale.

There are hopes that play round her, like fires on the
    mast,
That will light the dark hour till its danger has past;
There are prayers that will plead with the storm when
    it raves,
And whisper " Be still! " to the turbulent waves.

Nay, think not that Friendship has called us in vain
To join the fair ring ere we break it again;
There is strength in its circle, — you lose the bright
    star,
But its sisters still chain it, though shining afar.

I give you one health in the juice of the vine,
The blood of the vineyard shall mingle with mine;
Thus, thus let us drain the last dew-drops of gold,
As we empty our hearts of the blessings they hold.

April 29, 1855.

AT A BIRTHDAY FESTIVAL.

TO J. R. LOWELL.

We will not speak of years to-night, —
    For what have years to bring
But larger floods of love and light,
    And sweeter songs to sing?

We will not drown in wordy praise
    The kindly thoughts that rise;
If Friendship own one tender phrase,
    He reads it in our eyes.

We need not waste our schoolboy art
    To gild this notch of Time; —
Forgive me if my wayward heart
    Has throbbed in artless rhyme.

Enough for him the silent grasp
    That knits us hand in hand,
And he the bracelet's radiant clasp
    That locks our circling band.

Strength to his hours of manly toil!
    Peace to his starlit dreams!
Who loves alike the furrowed soil,
    The music-haunted streams!

Sweet smiles to keep forever bright
    The sunshine on his lips,
And faith that sees the ring of light
    Round nature's last eclipse!

February 22, 1859.

A BIRTHDAY TRIBUTE.

TO J. F. CLARKE.

Who is the shepherd sent to lead,
   Through pastures green, the Master's sheep?
What guileless " Israelite indeed "
   The folded flock may watch and keep?

He who with manliest spirit joins
   The heart of gentlest human mould,
With burning light and girded loins,
   To guide the flock, or watch the fold;

True to all Truth the world denies,
   Not tongue-tied for its gilded sin;
Not always right in all men's eyes,
   But faithful to the light within;

Who asks no meed of earthly fame,
    Who knows no earthly master's call,
Who hopes for man, through guilt and shame,
    Still answering, " God is over all; "

Who makes another's grief his own,
    Whose smile lends joy a double cheer ;
Where lives the saint, if such be known ? —
    Speak softly, — such an one is here !

O faithful shepherd ! thou hast borne
    The heat and burden of the day ;
Yet, o'er thee, bright with beams unshorn,
    The sun still shows thine onward way.

To thee our fragrant love we bring,
    In buds that April half displays,
Sweet first-born angels of the spring,
    Caught in their opening hymn of praise.

What though our faltering accents fail,
    Our captives know their message well,
Our words unbreathed their lips exhale,
    And sigh more love than ours can tell.

April 4, 1860.

THE GRAY CHIEF.

FOR THE MEETING OF THE MASSACHUSETTS MEDICAL SOCIETY, 1859.

'T is sweet to fight our battles o'er,
    And crown with honest praise
The gray old chief, who strikes no more
    The blow of better days.

Before the true and trusted sage
    With willing hearts we bend,
When years have touched with hallowing age
    Our Master, Guide, and Friend.

For all his manhood's labor past,
    For love and faith long tried,
His age is honored to the last,
    Though strength and will have died.

But when, untamed by toil and strife,
    Full in our front he stands,
The torch of light, the shield of life,
    Still lifted in his hands,

No temple, though its walls resound
    With bursts of ringing cheers,
Can hold the honors that surround
    His manhood's twice-told years!

THE LAST LOOK.

W. W. SWAIN.

Behold — not him we knew!
This was the prison which his soul looked through,
    Tender, and brave, and true.

His voice no more is heard;
And his dead name — that dear familiar word —
    Lies on our lips unstirred.

He spake with poet's tongue;
Living, for him the minstrel's lyre was strung:
    He shall not die unsung!

Grief tried his love, and pain;
And the long bondage of his martyr-chain
    Vexed his sweet soul, — in vain!

It felt life's surges break,
As, girt with stormy seas, his island lake,
    Smiling while tempests wake.

How can we sorrow more?
Grieve not for him whose heart had gone before
    To that untrodden shore!

Lo, through its leafy screen,
A gleam of sunlight on a ring of green,
    Untrodden, half unseen!

Here let his body rest,
Where the calm shadows that his soul loved best
    May slide above his breast.

Smooth his uncurtained bed;
And if some natural tears are softly shed,
    It is not for the dead.

Fold the green turf aright
For the long hours before the morning's light,
    And say the last Good Night!

And plant a clear white stone
Close by those mounds which hold his loved, his own, —
    Lonely, but not alone.

Here let him sleeping lie,
Till Heaven's bright watchers slumber in the sky,
    And Death himself shall die!

NAUSHON, September 22, 1858.

IN MEMORY OF

CHARLES WENTWORTH UPHAM, JUNIOR.

He was all sunshine; in his face
   The very soul of sweetness shone;
Fairest and gentlest of his race;
   None like him we can call our own.

Something there was of one that died
   In her fresh spring-time long ago,
Our first dear Mary, angel-eyed,
   Whose smile it was a bliss to know.

Something of her whose love imparts
   Such radiance to her day's decline,
We feel its twilight in our hearts
   Bright as the earliest morning-shine.

Yet richer strains our eye could trace
    That made our plainer mould more fair,
That curved the lip with happier grace,
    That waved the soft and silken hair.

Dust unto dust! the lips are still
    That only spoke to cheer and bless;
The folded hands lie white and chill
    Unclasped from sorrow's last caress.

Leave him in peace; he will not heed
    These idle tears we vainly pour,
Give back to earth the fading weed
    Of mortal shape his spirit wore.

"Shall I not weep my heartstrings torn,
    My flower of love that falls half blown,
My youth uncrowned, my life forlorn,
    A thorny path to walk alone?"

O Mary! one who bore thy name,
    Whose Friend and Master was divine,
Sat waiting silent till He came,
    Bowed down in speechless grief like thine.

"Where have ye laid him?" "Come," they say,
  Pointing to where the loved one slept;
Weeping, the sister led the way, —
  And, seeing Mary, "Jesus wept."

He weeps with thee, with all that mourn,
  And He shall wipe thy streaming eyes
Who knew all sorrows, woman-born, —
  Trust in his word; thy dead shall rise!

April 15, 1860.

MARTHA.

DIED JANUARY 7, 1861.

Sexton! Martha's dead and gone;
    Toll the bell! toll the bell!
Her weary hands their labor cease;
Good night, poor Martha, — sleep in peace!
    Toll the bell!

Sexton! Martha's dead and gone;
    Toll the bell! toll the bell!
For many a year has Martha said,
"I'm old and poor, — would I were dead!"
    Toll the bell!

Sexton! Martha's dead and gone;
    Toll the bell! toll the bell!
She'll bring no more, by day or night,
Her basket full of linen white.
    Toll the bell!

Sexton! Martha's dead and gone;
  Toll the bell! toll the bell!
'T is fitting she should lie below
A pure white sheet of drifted snow.
  Toll the bell!

Sexton! Martha's dead and gone;
  Toll the bell! toll the bell!
Sleep, Martha, sleep, to wake in light,
Where all the robes are stainless white.
  Toll the bell!

SUN AND SHADOW.

As I look from the isle, o'er its billows of green,
    To the billows of foam-crested blue,
Yon bark, that afar in the distance is seen,
    Half dreaming, my eyes will pursue:
Now dark in the shadow, she scatters the spray
    As the chaff in the stroke of the flail;
Now white as the sea-gull, she flies on her way,
    The sun gleaming bright on her sail.

Yet her pilot is thinking of dangers to shun,—
    Of breakers that whiten and roar;
How little he cares, if in shadow or sun
    They see him who gaze from the shore!
He looks to the beacon that looms from the reef,
    To the rock that is under his lee,
As he drifts on the blast, like a wind-wafted leaf,
    O'er the gulfs of the desolate sea.

Thus drifting afar to the dim-vaulted caves
    Where life and its ventures are laid,
The dreamers who gaze while we battle the waves
    May see us in sunshine or shade;
Yet true to our course, though our shadow grow dark,
    We'll trim our broad sail as before,
And stand by the rudder that governs the bark,
    Nor ask how we look from the shore!

THE CHAMBERED NAUTILUS.

This is the ship of pearl, which, poets feign,
    Sails the unshadowed main, —
    The venturous bark that flings
On the sweet summer wind its purpled wings
In gulfs enchanted, where the Siren sings,
    And coral reefs lie bare,
Where the cold sea-maids rise to sun their streaming hair.

Its webs of living gauze no more unfurl;
    Wrecked is the ship of pearl!
    And every chambered cell,
Where its dim dreaming life was wont to dwell,
As the frail tenant shaped his growing shell,
    Before thee lies revealed, —
Its irised ceiling rent, its sunless crypt unsealed!

Year after year beheld the silent toil
    That spread his lustrous coil;
    Still, as the spiral grew,
He left the past year's dwelling for the new,
Stole with soft step its shining archway through,
    Built up its idle door,
Stretched in his last-found home, and knew the old no more.

Thanks for the heavenly message brought by thee,
    Child of the wandering sea,
    Cast from her lap, forlorn!
From thy dead lips a clearer note is born
Than ever Triton blew from wreathéd horn!
    While on mine ear it rings,
Through the deep caves of thought I hear a voice that sings:—

Build thee more stately mansions, O my soul,
    As the swift seasons roll!
    Leave thy low-vaulted past!
Let each new temple, nobler than the last,
Shut thee from heaven with a dome more vast,
    Till thou at length art free,
Leaving thine outgrown shell by life's unresting sea!

THE TWO ARMIES.

As Life's unending column pours,
    Two marshalled hosts are seen, —
Two armies on the trampled shores
    That Death flows black between.

One marches to the drum-beat's roll,
    The wide-mouthed clarion's bray,
And bears upon a crimson scroll,
    "Our glory is to slay."

One moves in silence by the stream,
    With sad, yet watchful eyes,
Calm as the patient planet's gleam
    That walks the clouded skies.

Along its front no sabres shine,
   No blood-red pennons wave;
Its banner bears the single line,
   " Our duty is to save."

For those no death-bed's lingering shade;
   At Honor's trumpet-call,
With knitted brow and lifted blade
   In Glory's arms they fall.

For these no clashing falchions bright,
   No stirring battle-cry;
The bloodless stabber calls by night, —
   Each answers, " Here am I ! "

For those the sculptor's laurelled bust,
   The builder's marble piles,
The anthems pealing o'er their dust
   Through long cathedral aisles.

For these the blossom-sprinkled turf
   That floods the lonely graves,
When Spring rolls in her sea-green surf
   In flowery-foaming waves.

Two paths lead upward from below,
    And angels wait above,
Who count each burning life-drop's flow,
    Each falling tear of Love.

Though from the Hero's bleeding breast
    Her pulses Freedom drew,
Though the white lilies in her crest
    Sprang from that scarlet dew, —

While Valor's haughty champions wait
    Till all their scars are shown,
Love walks unchallenged through the gate,
    To sit beside the Throne!

FOR THE MEETING OF THE NATIONAL SANITARY ASSOCIATION.

1860.

WHAT makes the Healing Art divine?
   The bitter drug we buy and sell,
The brands that scorch, the blades that shine,
   The scars we leave, the "cures" we tell?

Are these thy glories, holiest Art, —
   The trophies that adorn thee best, —
Or but thy triumph's meanest part,
   Where mortal weakness stands confessed?

We take the arms that Heaven supplies
   For Life's long battle with Disease,
Taught by our various need to prize
   Our frailest weapons, even these.

But ah! when Science drops her shield —
   Its peaceful shelter proved in vain —
And bares her snow-white arm to wield
   The sad, stern ministry of pain;

When shuddering o'er the fount of life,
   She folds her heaven-anointed wings,
To lift unmoved the glittering knife
   That searches all its crimson springs;

When, faithful to her ancient lore,
   She thrusts aside her fragrant balm
For blistering juice, or cankering ore,
   And tames them till they cure or calm;

When in her gracious hand are seen
   The dregs and scum of earth and seas,
Her kindness counting all things clean
   That lend the sighing sufferer ease;

Though on the field that Death has won,
   She saves some stragglers in retreat; —
These single acts of mercy done
   Are but confessions of defeat.

What though our tempered poisons save
    Some wrecks of life from aches and ails:
Those grand specifics Nature gave
    Were never poised by weights or scales!

God lent his creatures light and air,
    And waters open to the skies;
Man locks him in a stifling lair,
    And wonders why his brother dies!

In vain our pitying tears are shed,
    In vain we rear the sheltering pile
Where Art weeds out from bed to bed
    The plagues we planted by the mile!

Be that the glory of the past;
    With these our sacred toils begin:
So flies in tatters from its mast
    The yellow flag of sloth and sin,

And lo! the starry folds reveal
    The blazoned truth we hold so dear:
To guard is better than to heal, —
    The shield is nobler than the spear!

MUSA.

O my lost Beauty! — hast thou folded quite
    Thy wings of morning light
    Beyond those iron gates
Where Life crowds hurrying to the haggard Fates,
And Age upon his mound of ashes waits
    To chill our fiery dreams,
Hot from the heart of youth plunged in his icy streams?

Leave me not fading in these weeds of care,
    Whose flowers are silvered hair!
    Have I not loved thee long,
Though my young lips have often done thee wrong,
And vexed thy heaven-tuned ear with careless song?
    Ah, wilt thou yet return,
Bearing thy rose-hued torch, and bid thine altar burn?

Come to me! — I will flood thy silent shrine
    With my soul's sacred wine,
    And heap thy marble floors
As the wild spice-trees waste their fragrant stores
In leafy islands walled with madrepores
    And lapped in Orient seas,
When all their feathery palms toss, plume-like, in the breeze.

Come to me! — thou shalt feed on honeyed words,
    Sweeter than song of birds; —
    No wailing bulbul's throat,
No melting dulcimer's melodious note,
When o'er the midnight wave its murmurs float,
    Thy ravished sense might soothe
With flow so liquid-soft, with strain so velvet-smooth.

Thou shalt be decked with jewels, like a queen,
    Sought in those bowers of green
    Where loop the clustered vines
And the close-clinging dulcamara* twines, —
Pure pearls of Maydew where the moonlight shines,

---

* The "bitter-sweet" of New England is the *Celastrus scandens*, — "Bourreau des arbres" of the Canadian French.

And Summer's fruited gems,
And coral pendants shorn from Autumn's berried
stems.

Sit by me drifting on the sleepy waves, —
    Or stretched by grass-grown graves,
    Whose gray, high-shouldered stones,
Carved with old names Life's time-worn roll disowns,
Lean, lichen-spotted, o'er the crumbled bones
    Still slumbering where they lay
While the sad Pilgrim watched to scare the wolf away.

Spread o'er my couch thy visionary wing!
    Still let me dream and sing, —
    Dream of that winding shore
Where scarlet cardinals bloom — for me no more, —
The stream with heaven beneath its liquid floor,
    And clustering nenuphars
Sprinkling its mirrored blue like golden-chaliced stars!

Come while their balms the linden-blossoms shed! —
    Come while the rose is red, —
    While blue-eyed Summer smiles
On the green ripples round yon sunken piles
Washed by the moon-wave warm from Indian isles,

      And on the sultry air
The chestnuts spread their palms like holy men in
        prayer !

O for thy burning lips to fire my brain
      With thrills of wild, sweet pain ! —
      On life's autumnal blast,
Like shrivelled leaves, youth's passion-flowers are cast, —
Once loving thee, we love thee to the last ! —
      Behold thy new-decked shrine,
And hear once more the voice that breathed " Forever
        thine ! "

THE VOICELESS.

We count the broken lyres that rest
   Where the sweet wailing singers slumber,
But o'er their silent sister's breast
   The wild-flowers who will stoop to number?
A few can touch the magic string,
   And noisy Fame is proud to win them; —
Alas for those that never sing,
   But die with all their music in them!

Nay, grieve not for the dead alone
   Whose song has told their hearts' sad story, —
Weep for the voiceless, who have known
   The cross without the crown of glory!
Not where Leucadian breezes sweep
   O'er Sappho's memory-haunted billow,
But where the glistening night-dews weep
   On nameless sorrow's churchyard pillow.

O hearts that break and give no sign
    Save whitening lip and fading tresses,
Till Death pours out his cordial wine
    Slow-dropped from Misery's crushing presses, —
If singing breath or echoing chord
    To every hidden pang were given,
What endless melodies were poured,
    As sad as earth, as sweet as heaven!

THE CROOKED FOOTPATH.

Ah, here it is! the sliding rail
   That marks the old remembered spot, —
The gap that struck our schoolboy trail, —
   The crooked path across the lot.

It left the road by school and church,
   A pencilled shadow, nothing more,
That parted from the silver birch
   And ended at the farm-house door.

No line or compass traced its plan;
   With frequent bends to left or right,
In aimless, wayward curves it ran,
   But always kept the door in sight.

The gabled porch, with woodbine green, —
    The broken millstone at the sill, —
Though many a rood might stretch between,
    The truant child could see them still.

No rocks across the pathway lie, —
    No fallen trunk is o'er it thrown, —
And yet it winds, we know not why,
    And turns as if for tree or stone.

Perhaps some lover trod the way
    With shaking knees and leaping heart, —
And so it often runs astray
    With sinuous sweep or sudden start.

Or one, perchance, with clouded brain
    From some unholy banquet reeled, —
And since, our devious steps maintain
    His track across the trodden field.

Nay, deem not thus, — no earthborn will
    Could ever trace a faultless line;
Our truest steps are human still, —
    To walk unswerving were divine!

Truants from love, we dream of wrath; —
O, rather let us trust the more!
Through all the wanderings of the path,
We still can see our Father's door!

THE TWO STREAMS.

    Behold the rocky wall
      That down its sloping sides
Pours the swift rain-drops, blending, as they fall,
      In rushing river-tides!

    Yon stream, whose sources run
      Turned by a pebble's edge,
Is Athabasca, rolling toward the sun
      Through the cleft mountain-ledge.

    The slender rill had strayed,
      But for the slanting stone,
To evening's ocean, with the tangled braid
      Of foam-flecked Oregon.

So from the heights of Will
Life's parting stream descends,
And, as a moment turns its slender rill,
Each widening torrent bends, —

From the same cradle's side,
From the same mother's knee, —
One to long darkness and the frozen tide,
One to the Peaceful Sea!

ROBINSON OF LEYDEN.

He sleeps not here; in hope and prayer
   His wandering flock had gone before,
But he, the shepherd, might not share
   Their sorrows on the wintry shore.

Before the Speedwell's anchor swung,
   Ere yet the Mayflower's sail was spread,
While round his feet the Pilgrims clung,
   The pastor spake, and thus he said: —

"Men, brethren, sisters, children dear!
   God calls you hence from over sea;
Ye may not build by Haerlem Meer,
   Nor yet along the Zuyder-Zee.

"Ye go to bear the saving word
  To tribes unnamed and shores untrod:
Heed well the lessons ye have heard
  From those old teachers taught of God.

"Yet think not unto them was lent
  All light for all the coming days,
And Heaven's eternal wisdom spent
  In making straight the ancient ways:

"The living fountain overflows
  For every flock, for every lamb,
Nor heeds, though angry creeds oppose
  With Luther's dike or Calvin's dam."

He spake: with lingering, long embrace,
  With tears of love and partings fond,
They floated down the creeping Maas,
  Along the isle of Ysselmond.

They passed the frowning towers of Briel,
  The "Hook of Holland's" shelf of sand,
And grated soon with lifting keel
  The sullen shores of Fatherland.

No home for these! — too well they knew
    The mitred king behind the throne; —
The sails were set, the pennons flew,
    And westward ho! for worlds unknown.

— And these were they who gave us birth,
    The Pilgrims of the sunset wave,
Who won for us this virgin earth,
    And freedom with the soil they gave.

The pastor slumbers by the Rhine, —
    In alien earth the exiles lie, —
Their nameless graves our holiest shrine,
    His words our noblest battle-cry!

Still cry them, and the world shall hear,
    Ye dwellers by the storm-swept sea!
Ye *have* not built by Haerlem Meer,
    Nor on the land-locked Zuyder-Zee!

SAINT ANTHONY THE REFORMER.

HIS TEMPTATION.

No fear lest praise should make us proud!
    We know how cheaply that is won;
The idle homage of the crowd
    Is proof of tasks as idly done.

A surface-smile may pay the toil
    That follows still the conquering Right,
With soft, white hands to dress the spoil
    That sun-browned valor clutched in fight.

Sing the sweet song of other days,
    Serenely placid, safely true,
And o'er the present's parching ways
    Thy verse distils like evening dew.

But speak in words of living power, —
    They fall like drops of scalding rain
That plashed before the burning shower
    Swept o'er the cities of the plain!

Then scowling Hate turns deadly pale, —
    Then Passion's half-coiled adders spring,
And, smitten through their leprous mail,
    Strike right and left in hope to sting.

If thou, unmoved by poisoning wrath,
    Thy feet on earth, thy heart above,
Canst walk in peace thy kingly path,
    Unchanged in trust, unchilled in love, —

Too kind for bitter words to grieve,
    Too firm for clamor to dismay,
When Faith forbids thee to believe,
    And Meekness calls to disobey, —

Ah, then beware of mortal pride!
    The smiling pride that calmly scorns
Those foolish fingers, crimson dyed
    In laboring on thy crown of thorns!

AVIS.

I MAY not rightly call thy name, —
    Alas! thy forehead never knew
The kiss that happier children claim,
    Nor glistened with baptismal dew.

Daughter of want and wrong and woe,
    I saw thee with thy sister-band,
Snatched from the whirlpool's narrowing flow
    By Mercy's strong yet trembling hand.

— "Avis!" — With Saxon eye and cheek,
    At once a woman and a child,
The saint uncrowned I came to seek
    Drew near to greet us, — spoke, and smiled.

God gave that sweet sad smile she wore
    All wrong to shame, all souls to win, —
A heavenly sunbeam sent before
    Her footsteps through a world of sin.

— "And who is Avis?" — Hear the tale
    The calm-voiced matrons gravely tell, —
The story known through all the vale
    Where Avis and her sisters dwell.

With the lost children running wild,
    Strayed from the hand of human care,
They find one little refuse child
    Left helpless in its poisoned lair.

The primal mark is on her face, —
    The chattel-stamp, — the pariah-stain
That follows still her hunted race, —
    The curse without the crime of Cain.

How shall our smooth-turned phrase relate
    The little suffering outcast's ail?
Not Lazarus at the rich man's gate
    So turned the rose-wreathed revellers pale.

Ah, veil the living death from sight
    That wounds our beauty-loving eye!
The children turn in selfish fright,
    The white-lipped nurses hurry by.

Take her, dread Angel! Break in love
    This bruisèd reed and make it thine! —
No voice descended from above,
    But Avis answered, " She is mine."

The task that dainty menials spurn
    The fair young girl has made her own;
Her heart shall teach, her hand shall learn,
    The toils, the duties yet unknown.

So Love and Death in lingering strife
    Stand face to face from day to day,
Still battling for the spoil of Life
    While the slow seasons creep away.

Love conquers Death; the prize is won;
    See to her joyous bosom pressed
The dusky daughter of the sun, —
    The bronze against the marble breast!

Her task is done ; no voice divine
  Has crowned her deeds with saintly fame.
No eye can see the aureole shine
  That rings her brow with heavenly flame.

Yet what has holy page more sweet,
  Or what had woman's love more fair,
When Mary clasped her Saviour's feet
  With flowing eyes and streaming hair?

Meek child of sorrow, walk unknown,
  The Angel of that earthly throng,
And let thine image live alone
  To hallow this unstudied song!

IRIS, HER BOOK.

I PRAY thee by the soul of her that bore thee,
By thine own sister's spirit I implore thee,
Deal gently with the leaves that lie before thee!

For Iris had no mother to infold her,
Nor ever leaned upon a sister's shoulder,
Telling the twilight thoughts that Nature told her.

She had not learned the mystery of awaking
Those chorded keys that soothe a sorrow's aching,
Giving the dumb heart voice, that else were breaking.

Yet lived, wrought, suffered. Lo, the pictured token!
Why should her fleeting day-dreams fade unspoken,
Like daffodils that die with sheaths unbroken?

She knew not love, yet lived in maiden fancies, —
Walked simply clad, a queen of high romances,
And talked strange tongues with angels in her trances.

Twin-souled she seemed, a twofold nature wearing, —
Sometimes a flashing falcon in her daring,
Then a poor mateless dove that droops despairing.

Questioning all things: Why her Lord had sent her?
What were these torturing gifts, and wherefore lent her?
Scornful as spirit fallen, its own tormentor.

And then all tears and anguish: Queen of Heaven,
Sweet Saints, and Thou by mortal sorrows riven,
Save me! O, save me! Shall I die forgiven?

And then —— Ah, God! But nay, it little matters:
Look at the wasted seeds that autumn scatters,
The myriad germs that Nature shapes and shatters!

If she had —— Well! She longed, and knew not
    wherefore.
Had the world nothing she might live to care for?
No second self to say her evening prayer for?

She knew the marble shapes that set men dreaming,
Yet with her shoulders bare and tresses streaming
Showed not unlovely to her simple seeming.

Vain? Let it be so! Nature was her teacher.
What if a lonely and unsistered creature
Loved her own harmless gift of pleasing feature,

Saying, unsaddened, — This shall soon be faded,
And double-hued the shining tresses braided,
And all the sunlight of the morning shaded?

—— This her poor book is full of saddest follies,
Of tearful smiles and laughing melancholies,
With summer roses twined and wintry hollies.

In the strange crossing of uncertain chances,
Somewhere, beneath some maiden's tear-dimmed glances
May fall her little book of dreams and fancies.

Sweet sister! Iris, who shall never name thee,
Trembling for fear her open heart may shame thee,
Speaks from this vision-haunted page to claim thee.

Spare her, I pray thee! If the maid is sleeping,
Peace with her! she has had her hour of weeping.
No more! She leaves her memory in thy keeping.

UNDER THE VIOLETS.

Her hands are cold; her face is white;
   No more her pulses come and go;
Her eyes are shut to life and light; —
   Fold the white vesture, snow on snow,
   And lay her where the violets blow.

But not beneath a graven stone,
   To plead for tears with alien eyes;
A slender cross of wood alone
   Shall say, that here a maiden lies
   In peace beneath the peaceful skies.

And gray old trees of hugest limb
   Shall wheel their circling shadows round
To make the scorching sunlight dim
   That drinks the greenness from the ground,
   And drop their dead leaves on her mound.

When o'er their boughs the squirrels run,
    And through their leaves the robins call,
And, ripening in the autumn sun,
    The acorns and the chestnuts fall,
    Doubt not that she will heed them all.

For her the morning choir shall sing
    Its matins from the branches high,
And every minstrel-voice of Spring,
    That trills beneath the April sky,
    Shall greet her with its earliest cry.

When, turning round their dial-track,
    Eastward the lengthening shadows pass,
Her little mourners, clad in black,
    The crickets, sliding through the grass,
    Shall pipe for her an evening mass.

At last the rootlets of the trees
    Shall find the prison where she lies,
And bear the buried dust they seize
    In leaves and blossoms to the skies.
    So may the soul that warmed it rise!

If any, born of kindlier blood,
   Should ask, What maiden lies below?
Say only this: A tender bud,
   That tried to blossom in the snow,
   Lies withered where the violets blow.

THE PROMISE.

Not charity we ask,
    Nor yet thy gift refuse;
Please thy light fancy with the easy task
    Only to look and choose.

The little-heeded toy
    That wins thy treasured gold
May be the dearest memory, holiest joy,
    Of coming years untold.

Heaven rains on every heart,
    But there its showers divide,
The drops of mercy choosing as they part
    The dark or glowing side.

One kindly deed may turn
    The fountain of thy soul
To love's sweet day-star, that shall o'er thee burn
    Long as its currents roll!

The pleasures thou hast planned, —
    Where shall their memory be
When the white angel with the freezing hand
    Shall sit and watch by thee?

Living, thou dost not live,
    If mercy's spring run dry;
What Heaven has lent thee wilt thou freely give,
    Dying, thou shalt not die!

He promised even so!
    To thee His lips repeat, —
Behold, the tears that soothed thy sister's woe
    Have washed thy Master's feet!

March 20, 1859.

THE LIVING TEMPLE.

Not in the world of light alone,
Where God has built his blazing throne,
Nor yet alone in earth below,
With belted seas that come and go,
And endless isles of sunlit green,
Is all thy Maker's glory seen:
Look in upon thy wondrous frame,—
Eternal wisdom still the same!

The smooth, soft air with pulse-like waves
Flows murmuring through its hidden caves,
Whose streams of brightening purple rush,
Fired with a new and livelier blush,
While all their burden of decay
The ebbing current steals away,
And red with Nature's flame they start
From the warm fountains of the heart.

No rest that throbbing slave may ask,
Forever quivering o'er his task,
While far and wide a crimson jet
Leaps forth to fill the woven net
Which in unnumbered crossing tides
The flood of burning life divides,
Then, kindling each decaying part,
Creeps back to find the throbbing heart.

But warmed with that unchanging flame
Behold the outward moving frame,
Its living marbles jointed strong
With glistening band and silvery thong,
And linked to reason's guiding reins
By myriad rings in trembling chains,
Each graven with the threaded zone
Which claims it as the master's own.

See how yon beam of seeming white
Is braided out of seven-hued light,
Yet in those lucid globes no ray
By any chance shall break astray.
Hark how the rolling surge of sound,
Arches and spirals circling round,
Wakes the hushed spirit through thine ear
With music it is heaven to hear.

Then mark the cloven sphere that holds
All thought in its mysterious folds,
That feels sensation's faintest thrill,
And flashes forth the sovereign will;
Think on the stormy world that dwells
Locked in its dim and clustering cells!
The lightning gleams of power it sheds
Along its hollow glassy threads!

O Father! grant thy love divine
To make these mystic temples thine!
When wasting age and wearying strife
Have sapped the leaning walls of life,
When darkness gathers over all,
And the last tottering pillars fall,
Take the poor dust thy mercy warms,
And mould it into heavenly forms!

HYMN OF TRUST.

O LOVE Divine, that stooped to share
    Our sharpest pang, our bitterest tear,
On Thee we cast each earth-born care,
    We smile at pain while Thou art near!

Though long the weary way we tread,
    And sorrow crown each lingering year,
No path we shun, no darkness dread,
    Our hearts still whispering, Thou art near!

When drooping pleasure turns to grief,
    And trembling faith is changed to fear,
The murmuring wind, the quivering leaf,
    Shall softly tell us, Thou art near!

On Thee we fling our burdening woe,
O Love Divine, forever dear,
Content to suffer while we know,
Living and dying, Thou art near!

A SUN-DAY HYMN.

Lord of all being! throned afar,
Thy glory flames from sun and star;
Centre and soul of every sphere,
Yet to each loving heart how near!

Sun of our life, thy quickening ray
Sheds on our path the glow of day;
Star of our hope, thy softened light
Cheers the long watches of the night.

Our midnight is thy smile withdrawn;
Our noontide is thy gracious dawn;
Our rainbow arch thy mercy's sign;
All, save the clouds of sin, are thine!

A SUN-DAY HYMN.

Lord of all life, below, above,
Whose light is truth, whose warmth is love,
Before thy ever-blazing throne
We ask no lustre of our own.

Grant us thy truth to make us free,
And kindling hearts that burn for thee,
Till all thy living altars claim
One holy light, one heavenly flame!

A VOICE OF THE LOYAL NORTH.

NATIONAL FAST, JANUARY 4, 1861.

We sing "Our Country's" song to-night
   With saddened voice and eye;
Her banner droops in clouded light
   Beneath the wintry sky.
We'll pledge her once in golden wine
   Before her stars have set:
Though dim one reddening orb may shine,
   We have a Country yet.

'T were vain to sigh o'er errors past,
   The fault of sires or sons;
Our soldier heard the threatening blast,
   And spiked his useless guns;
He saw the star-wreathed ensign fall,
   By mad invaders torn;
But saw it from the bastioned wall
   That laughed their rage to scorn!

What though their angry cry is flung
    Across the howling wave, —
They smite the air with idle tongue
    The gathering storm who brave;
Enough of speech! the trumpet rings;
    Be silent, patient, calm, —
God help them if the tempest swings
    The pine against the palm!

Our toilsome years have made us tame;
    Our strength has slept unfelt;
The furnace-fire is slow to flame
    That bids our ploughshares melt;
'T is hard to lose the bread they win
    In spite of Nature's frowns, —
To drop the iron threads we spin
    That weave our web of towns,

To see the rusting turbines stand
    Before the emptied flumes,
To fold the arms that flood the land
    With rivers from their looms, —
But harder still for those who learn
    The truth forgot so long;
When once their slumbering passions burn,
    The peaceful are the strong!

The Lord have mercy on the weak,
   And calm their frenzied ire,
And save our brothers ere they shriek,
   "We played with Northern fire!"
The eagle hold his mountain height, —
   The tiger pace his den!
Give all their country, each his right!
   God keep us all! Amen!

BROTHER JONATHAN'S LAMENT FOR SISTER CAROLINE.

She has gone,—she has left us in passion and pride,—
Our stormy-browed sister, so long at our side!
She has torn her own star from our firmament's glow,
And turned on her brother the face of a foe!

O Caroline, Caroline, child of the sun,
We can never forget that our hearts have been one,—
Our foreheads both sprinkled in Liberty's name,
From the fountain of blood with the finger of flame!

You were always too ready to fire at a touch;
But we said, "She is hasty,—she does not mean much."
We have scowled, when you uttered some turbulent threat;
But Friendship still whispered, "Forgive and forget!"

Has our love all died out? Have its altars grown cold?
Has the curse come at last which the fathers foretold?
Then Nature must teach us the strength of the chain
That her petulant children would sever in vain.

They may fight till the buzzards are gorged with their
    spoil,
Till the harvest grows black as it rots in the soil,
Till the wolves and the catamounts troop from their
    caves,
And the shark tracks the pirate, the lord of the waves:

In vain is the strife! When its fury is past,
Their fortunes must flow in one channel at last,
As the torrents that rush from the mountains of snow
Roll mingled in peace through the valleys below.

Our Union is river, lake, ocean, and sky:
Man breaks not the medal, when God cuts the die!
Though darkened with sulphur, though cloven with
    steel,
The blue arch will brighten, the waters will heal!

O Caroline, Caroline, child of the sun,
There are battles with Fate that can never be won!

The star-flowering banner must never be furled,
For its blossoms of light are the hope of the world!

Go, then, our rash sister! afar and aloof,
Run wild in the sunshine away from our roof;
But when your heart aches and your feet have grown
    sore,
Remember the pathway that leads to our door!

  March 25, 1861.

UNDER THE WASHINGTON ELM, CAMBRIDGE.

April 27, 1861.

Eighty years have passed, and more,
    Since under the brave old tree
Our fathers gathered in arms, and swore
They would follow the sign their banners bore,
    And fight till the land was free.

Half of their work was done,
    Half is left to do, —
Cambridge, and Concord, and Lexington!
When the battle is fought and won,
    What shall be told of you?

Hark! — 't is the south-wind moans, —
    Who are the martyrs down?
Ah, the marrow was true in your children's bones
That sprinkled with blood the cursed stones
    Of the murder-haunted town!

What if the storm-clouds blow?
What if the green leaves fall?
Better the crashing tempest's throe
Than the army of worms that gnawed below;
Trample them one and all!

Then, when the battle is won,
And the land from traitors free,
Our children shall tell of the strife begun
When Liberty's second April sun
Was bright on our brave old tree!

INTERNATIONAL ODE.

OUR FATHERS' LAND.*

God bless our Fathers' Land!
Keep her in heart and hand
　　One with our own!
From all her foes defend,
Be her brave People's Friend,
On all her realms descend,
　　Protect her Throne!

Father, with loving care
Guard Thou her kingdom's Heir,
　　Guide all his ways:

---

* Sung in unison by twelve hundred children of the public schools, at the visit of the Prince of Wales to Boston, October 18, 1860. Air, "God save the Queen."

Thine arm his shelter be,
From him by land and sea
Bid storm and danger flee,
    Prolong his days!

Lord, let War's tempest cease,
Fold the whole Earth in peace
    Under thy wings!
Make all Thy nations one,
All hearts beneath the sun,
Till Thou shalt reign alone,
    Great King of kings!

FREEDOM, OUR QUEEN.

Land where the banners wave last in the sun,
Blazoned with star-clusters, many in one,
Floating o'er prairie and mountain and sea;
Hark! 't is the voice of thy children to thee!

Here at thine altar our vows we renew
Still in thy cause to be loyal and true, —
True to thy flag on the field and the wave,
Living to honor it, dying to save!

Mother of heroes! if perfidy's blight
Fall on a star in thy garland of light,
Sound but one bugle-blast! Lo! at the sign
Armies all panoplied wheel into line!

Hope of the world! thou hast broken its chains, —
Wear thy bright arms while a tyrant remains,
Stand for the right till the nations shall own
Freedom their sovereign, with Law for her throne!

Freedom! sweet Freedom! our voices resound,
Queen by God's blessing, unsceptred, uncrowned!
Freedom, sweet Freedom, our pulses repeat,
Warm with her life-blood, as long as they beat!

Fold the broad banner-stripes over her breast, —
Crown her with star-jewels Queen of the West!
Earth for her heritage, God for her friend,
She shall reign over us, world without end!

ARMY HYMN.

"Old Hundred."

O Lord of Hosts! Almighty King!
Behold the sacrifice we bring!
To every arm Thy strength impart,
Thy spirit shed through every heart!

Wake in our breasts the living fires,
The holy faith that warmed our sires;
Thy hand hath made our Nation free;
To die for her is serving Thee.

Be Thou a pillared flame to show
The midnight snare, the silent foe;
And when the battle thunders loud,
Still guide us in its moving cloud.

God of all Nations! Sovereign Lord!
In Thy dread name we draw the sword,
We lift the starry flag on high
That fills with light our stormy sky.

From treason's rent, from murder's stain,
Guard Thou its folds till Peace shall reign,—
Till fort and field, till shore and sea,
Join our loud anthem, PRAISE TO THEE!

PARTING HYMN.

"Dundee."

Father of Mercies, Heavenly Friend,
    We seek Thy gracious throne;
To Thee our faltering prayers ascend,
    Our fainting hearts are known!

From blasts that chill, from suns that smite,
    From every plague that harms;
In camp and march, in siege and fight,
    Protect our men-at-arms!

Though from our darkened lives they take
    What makes our life most dear,
We yield them for their country's sake
    With no relenting tear.

Our blood their flowing veins will shed,
    Their wounds our breasts will share;
O, save us from the woes we dread,
    Or grant us strength to bear!

Let each unhallowed cause that brings
    The stern destroyer cease,
Thy flaming angel fold his wings,
    And seraphs whisper Peace!

Thine are the sceptre and the sword,
    Stretch forth Thy mighty hand, —
Reign Thou our kingless nation's Lord,
    Rule Thou our throneless land!

THE FLOWER OF LIBERTY.

WHAT flower is this that greets the morn,
Its hues from Heaven so freshly born?
With burning star and flaming band
It kindles all the sunset land:
O tell us what its name may be,—
Is this the Flower of Liberty?
   It is the banner of the free,
    The starry Flower of Liberty.

In savage Nature's far abode
Its tender seed our fathers sowed;
The storm-winds rocked its swelling bud,
Its opening leaves were streaked with blood,
Till lo! earth's tyrants shook to see
The full-blown Flower of Liberty!
   Then hail the banner of the free,
    The starry Flower of Liberty.

Behold its streaming rays unite,
One mingling flood of braided light, —
The red that fires the Southern rose,
With spotless white from Northern snows,
And, spangled o'er its azure, see
The sister Stars of Liberty!
   Then hail the banner of the free,
   The starry Flower of Liberty!

The blades of heroes fence it round,
Where'er it springs is holy ground;
From tower and dome its glories spread;
It waves where lonely sentries tread;
It makes the land as ocean free,
And plants an empire on the sea!
   Then hail the banner of the free,
   The starry Flower of Liberty.

Thy sacred leaves, fair Freedom's flower,
Shall ever float on dome and tower,
To all their heavenly colors true,
In blackening frost or crimson dew, —
And God love us as we love thee,
Thrice holy Flower of Liberty!
   Then hail the banner of the free,
   The starry FLOWER OF LIBERTY.

THE SWEET LITTLE MAN.

DEDICATED TO THE STAY-AT-HOME RANGERS.

Now, while our soldiers are fighting our battles,
    Each at his post to do all that he can,
Down among rebels and contraband chattels,
    What are you doing, my sweet little man?

All the brave boys under canvas are sleeping,
    All of them pressing to march with the van,
Far from the home where their sweethearts are weeping;
    What are you waiting for, sweet little man?

You with the terrible warlike moustaches,
    Fit for a colonel or chief of a clan,
You with the waist made for sword-belts and sashes,
    Where are your shoulder-straps, sweet little man?

Bring him the buttonless garment of woman!
  Cover his face lest it freckle and tan;
Muster the Apron-string Guards on the Common,
  That is the corps for the sweet little man!

Give him for escort a file of young misses,
  Each of them armed with a deadly rattan;
They shall defend him from laughter and hisses,
  Aimed by low boys at the sweet little man.

All the fair maidens about him shall cluster,
  Pluck the white feathers from bonnet and fan,
Make him a plume like a turkey-wing duster,—
  That is the crest for the sweet little man!

O, but the Apron-string Guards are the fellows!
  Drilling each day since our troubles began,—
"Handle your walking-sticks!" "Shoulder umbrellas!"
  That is the style for the sweet little man.

Have we a nation to save? In the first place
  Saving ourselves is the sensible plan,—
Surely the spot where there's shooting's the worst place
  Where I can stand, says the sweet little man.

Catch me confiding my person with strangers!
　　Think how the cowardly Bull-Runners ran!
In the brigade of the Stay-at-home Rangers
　　Marches my corps, says the sweet little man.

Such was the stuff of the Malakoff-takers,
　　Such were the soldiers that scaled the Redan;
Truculent housemaids and bloodthirsty Quakers,
　　Brave not the wrath of the sweet little man!

Yield him the sidewalk, ye nursery maidens!
　　Sauve qui peut! Bridget, and right about! Ann;—
Fierce as a shark in a school of menhadens,
　　See him advancing, the sweet little man!

When the red flails of the battle-field's threshers
　　Beat out the continent's wheat from its bran,
While the wind scatters the chaffy seceshers,
　　What will become of our sweet little man?

When the brown soldiers come back from the borders,
　　How will he look while his features they scan?
How will he feel when he gets marching orders,
　　Signed by his lady love? sweet little man!

Fear not for him, though the rebels expect him, —
    Life is too precious to shorten its span;
Woman her broomstick shall raise to protect him,
    Will she not fight for the sweet little man!

Now then, nine cheers for the Stay-at-home Ranger!
    Blow the great fish-horn and beat the big pan!
First in the field that is farthest from danger,
    Take your white-feather plume, sweet little man!

VIVE LA FRANCE!

A SENTIMENT OFFERED AT THE DINNER TO H. I. H. THE PRINCE NAPOLEON, AT THE REVERE HOUSE, SEPT. 25, 1861.

The land of sunshine and of song!
   Her name your hearts divine;
To her the banquet's vows belong
   Whose breasts have poured its wine;
Our trusty friend, our true ally
   Through varied change and chance:
So, fill your flashing goblets high, —
   I give you, VIVE LA FRANCE!

Above our hosts in triple folds
   The self-same colors spread,
Where Valor's faithful arm upholds
   The blue, the white, the red;
Alike each nation's glittering crest
   Reflects the morning's glance, —
Twin eagles, soaring east and west:
   Once more, then, VIVE LA FRANCE!

Sister in trial! who shall count
    Thy generous friendship's claim,
Whose blood ran mingling in the fount
    That gave our land its name,
Till Yorktown saw in blended line
    Our conquering arms advance,
And victory's double garlands twine
    Our banners? VIVE LA FRANCE!

O land of heroes! in our need
    One gift from Heaven we crave
To stanch these wounds that vainly bleed, —
    The wise to lead the brave!
Call back one Captain of thy past
    From glory's marble trance,
Whose name shall be a bugle-blast
    To rouse us! VIVE LA FRANCE!

Pluck Condé's baton from the trench,
    Wake up stout Charles Martel,
Or find some woman's hand to clench
    The sword of La Pucelle!
Give us one hour of old Turenne, —
    One lift of Bayard's lance, —
Nay, call Marengo's Chief again
    To lead us! VIVE LA FRANCE!

Ah, hush! our welcome Guest shall hear
    But sounds of peace and joy;
No angry echo vex thine ear,
    Fair Daughter of Savoy!
Once more! the land of arms and arts,
    Of glory, grace, romance;
Her love lies warm in all our hearts:
    God bless her! VIVE LA FRANCE!

UNION AND LIBERTY.

FLAG of the heroes who left us their glory,
    Borne through their battle-fields' thunder and flame,
Blazoned in song and illumined in story,
    Wave o'er us all who inherit their fame!
        Up with our banner bright,
        Sprinkled with starry light,
    Spread its fair emblems from mountain to shore,
        While through the sounding sky
        Loud rings the Nation's cry, —
UNION AND LIBERTY! ONE EVERMORE!

Light of our firmament, guide of our Nation,
    Pride of her children, and honored afar,
Let the wide beams of thy full constellation
    Scatter each cloud that would darken a star!
        Up with our banner bright, etc.

Empire unsceptred! what foe shall assail thee,
  Bearing the standard of Liberty's van?
Think not the God of thy fathers shall fail thee,
  Striving with men for the birthright of man!
      Up with our banner bright, etc.

Yet if, by madness and treachery blighted,
  Dawns the dark hour when the sword thou must draw,
Then with the arms of thy millions united,
  Smite the bold traitors to Freedom and Law!
      Up with our banner bright, etc.

Lord of the Universe! shield us and guide us,
  Trusting thee always, through shadow and sun!
Thou hast united us, who shall divide us?
  Keep us, O keep us the MANY IN ONE!
      Up with our banner bright,
      Sprinkled with starry light,
  Spread its fair emblems from mountain to shore,
      While through the sounding sky
      Loud rings the Nation's cry,—
  UNION AND LIBERTY! ONE EVERMORE!

NOTE TO "AGNES."

THE story of Sir Harry Frankland and Agnes Surraige is told in the ballad with a very strict adhesion to the facts. These were obtained from information afforded me by the Reverend Mr. Webster of Hopkinton, in company with whom I visited the Frankland Mansion in that town, then standing; from a very interesting Memoir, by the Reverend Elias Nason of Medford, not yet published; and from the manuscript diary of Sir Harry, or more properly Sir Charles Henry Frankland, now in the library of the Massachusetts Historical Society.

At the time of the visit referred to, old Julia was living,* and on our return we called at the house where she resided. Her account is little more than paraphrased in the poem. If the incidents are treated with a certain liberality at the close of the fifth part, the essential fact that Agnes rescued Sir Harry from the ruins after the earthquake, and their subsequent marriage as related, may be accepted as literal truth. So with regard to most of the trifling details which are given; they are taken from the record.

It is to be hoped that the Reverend Mr. Nason's Memoir

* She is living now, June 10th, 1861.

will be published, that this extraordinary romance of our sober New England life may become familiar to that class of readers who prefer a rigorous statement to an embellished narrative. It will be found to contain many historical facts and allusions which add much to its romantic interest.

It is greatly to be regretted that the Frankland Mansion no longer exists. It was accidentally burned on the 23d of January, 1858, a year or two after the first sketch of this ballad was written. A visit to it was like stepping out of the century into the years before the Revolution. A new house, similar in plan and arrangements to the old one, has been built upon its site, and the terraces, the clump of box, and the lilacs, doubtless remain to bear witness to the truth of this story.

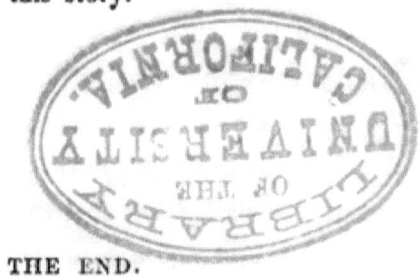

THE END.

Cambridge: Stereotyped and Printed by Welch, Bigelow, & Co.

www.ingramcontent.com/pod-product-compliance
Lightning Source LLC
Chambersburg PA
CBHW022023240426
43667CB00042B/1064